Brilliant Imperfection

Brilliant

Imperfection

Grappling with Cure

ELI CLARE

Duke University Press *Durham and London* 2017

Library of Congress Cataloging-in-Publication Data
Names: Clare, Eli, author.
Title: Brilliant imperfection : grappling with cure /
Eli Clare.
Description: Durham : Duke University Press, 2017. |
Includes bibliographical references and index.
Identifiers:
LCCN 2016030259 (print)
LCCN 2016031243 (ebook)
ISBN 9780822362760 (hardcover : alk. paper)
ISBN 9780822362876 (pbk. : alk. paper)
ISBN 9780822373520 (e-book)
Subjects: LCSH: People with disabilities. | Disabilities. |
Healing.
Classification: LCC HV1568.C528 2017 (print) | LCC HV1568
(ebook) | DDC 305.9/08—dc23
LC record available at https://lccn.loc.gov/2016030259

To the tallgrass prairie

and the crip communities

that have sustained me.

CONTENTS

ACKNOWLEDGMENTS

In different forms, earlier versions of the following pieces appeared in a variety of anthologies, journals, and periodicals:

"Airports and Cornfields," "Birthmark," "Body-Mind Yearning," "Cautionary Tale," "Living with *Monkey*," "*Normal* and *Natural*," "The Restoration of Health," "Walking in the Prairie," "Walking in the Prairie Again," "Wanting Cure," "Wishing You Less Pain," and "Yearning for the Peeper Pond" in *Material Ecocriticism*

"Ashley's Father" in *Tikkun*

"Cerebral Palsy" in *Writing the Walls Down: A Convergence of LGBTQ Voices*

"Carrie Buck I: Yearning," "Carrie Buck II: Torrent of History," and "Carrie Buck III: Feebleminded" in the *Journal of Literary and Cultural Disability Studies*

"Gender Transition" in *The Transgender Studies Reader 2*

"Shame and Pride" in the *Seattle Journal for Social Justice*

....

So many people contributed to this book I don't know where to begin. Editor extraordinaire and my first reader for the last twenty-five years, Joe Kadi has listened, urged me along, edited and reedited, and kept me grounded since the very first moments of this project. Susan Burch and I have met twice a month for more than two years, reading and supporting each other's writing projects. With generosity and brilliance, she has given me endless feedback, pushed, nudged, kept me accountable, and invited me to strengthen and clarify my ideas. Sebastian Margaret helped me develop all the central ideas in this book, supporting and encouraging me in countless ways. Mel Chen and Alison Kafer workshopped the manuscript at a crucial moment, helping me envision its final shape. My sweetie, Samuel Lurie, put up with me for the eleven-plus years I've been working on this project, talking through ideas, bringing me treats, and holding me.

Alison Kafer, Gabriel Arkels, Jade Brooks, Joe Kadi, Mel Chen, Michelle Jarman, Rebecca Widom, Samuel Lurie, Sebastian Margaret, Susan Burch, and Susan Raffo all read and listened to the manuscript in various stages of disarray, contributing greatly to the finished book. In addition, the whole project was supported by dozens of people in dozens of ways. Some helped me clarify and focus my thinking; others pointed me in new directions; still others gave me a necessary nudge at the exact right moment. Among them are Alexander John Goodrum, Angela Carter, Annette Marcus, Aura Glaser, Aurora Levins Morales, Chris Bell, Corbett O'Toole, Cory Silverberg, Diana Courvant, Ellen Samuels, Eunjung Kim, Gloria Thomas, Karen Kerns, Kim Nielsen, Laura Hershey, Loree Erickson, Patricia Fontaine, Patty Berne, Robin Stephens, Sue Schweik, and Sunaura Taylor.

I wrote this book as I sat in queer, trans, and disability communities and worked in multiracial, queer and trans people-of-color-led activist spaces. A big, big thank you for all the meetings, meals, walks/rolls, conversations, ideas, and aha moments to Aaron Ambrose, Alice Shepard, Amber Hollibaugh, Curtis Walker, Dean Spade, Denise Roy, Emi Koyama, Erick Fabris, Ethan Young, Heather MacAllister, Ibby Grace, Jake Pyne, Jay Sennett, Julio Orta, Laura Rauscher, Leah Dolmage, Leah Lakshmi Piepzna-Samarasinha, Lenny Olin, Leroy Moore, Lezlie Frye, Lisa Weiner-Mahfuz, Margaret Price, Mia Mingus, Nirmala Erevelles, Owen Daniel-McCarter, Riva Lehrer, Susan Stinson, Syrus Ware, Toby MacNutt, and Trishala Deb. My activist home bases while I wrote—the Disability Justice Collective and the ROOTS Collective—fed me in so many ways. A big shout out to everyone in both of those groups.

So much love, friendship, and encouragement makes my writing possible. Many thanks to Adrianne Neff, Alison Kafer, Annette Marcus, Deirdre Kelly, Gabriel Arkels, Heba Nimr, Joe Kadi, Loree Erickson, Lynne Whitney, Mel Chen, Merri Rose, Patricia Fontaine, Rebecca Widom, Samuel Lurie, Sarah Paige, Sebastian Margaret, Susan Burch, Susan Cowling, Susan Raffo, and Tammie Johnson for all your sustenance.

And finally, this book wouldn't have happened without the time and space I found at a residency at the Blue Mountain Center in the Adirondack Mountains and self-made writing retreats at Button Bay State Park and Ricker Pond State Park, both in Vermont. Endless gratitude to the trees and rocks, water and sky.

INTRODUCTION:
WRITING A MOSAIC

Meandering through a working-class neighborhood in Chicago, I happen upon a mosaic spread across the front of a community center. The colors catch me; purple, lavender, yellow, orange dance together. Up close the tiles are smooth, jagged, rounded, reflective, translucent, sparkling in the morning sun, no two pieces the same size and shape.

When I set out to write about cure more than a decade ago, I didn't intend to create a swirling, multibranched pattern of histories, ideas, and feelings. I planned to craft a half dozen interlocking essays. I imagined a simple, well-laid-out collage. But as so often happens with creative projects, I've ended up somewhere I never envisioned. I wrote a mosaic.

The fragments and slivers that make up this book came to me in my fury about eugenic practices, the words *defect* and *monkey*, the destruction of tallgrass prairie. They took shape as more than one disability activist challenged my fierce anti-cure politics. They emerged as I sifted through my own experiences with the diagnoses of mental retardation, cerebral palsy, schizophrenia, and gender identity disorder.

Everything in this mosaic started as a conversation. I drew on disability politics, antiracist activism, queer and transgender movement building, fat liberation work. I pulled environmental justice and reproductive justice into the fray. I used what I know firsthand about ableism and how it interlocks with racism, sexism, homophobia, transphobia, and classism.

I followed the lead of many communities and spiritual traditions that recognize body and mind not as two entities but as one, resisting the dualism built into white Western culture. Some use the word *bodymind* or *mindbody*; others choose *body/mind* or *body-and-mind*. I settled on *body-mind* in order to recognize both the inextricable relationships between our bodies and our minds and the ways in which the ideology of cure operates as if the two are distinct—the mind superior to the body, the mind defining personhood, the mind separating humans from nonhumans.

I trail my fingers along the mosaic, feeling bumps and ridges, the tiles' rough edges, almost sharp. And then I step back to the curb. The individual shapes become less distinct, and a woman's face, a boy in a handstand, feet akimbo, a hand holding a paintbrush emerge. They are vibrant, fractured, whole.

I started to see the patterns among these seemingly disconnected fragments and slivers as I talked late at night with friends hunkered around kitchen tables; watched the maple trees outside my writing room, season after season; and slept outside, sheltered by white pines.

But cure is slippery. Every place I began turned into a hundred new beginnings. I uncovered cure in obvious places: the Muscular Dystrophy Association's fund-raising appeals, the rhetoric of actor and wheelchair user Christopher Reeve as he lobbied for stem cell research and searched for a way to walk again. But it also kept appearing in less obvious places: ex-gay conversion therapy, weight loss surgery, and skin lightening creams marketed to dark-skinned women of color. I heard its echoes in ads for products claiming to remove women's facial hair and felt its reverberations in the medical technology some transgender people use to reshape our gendered and sexed body-minds. I saw it embedded in understandings of *normal* and *abnormal*, *natural* and *unnatural*, in stereotypes about disabled and chronically ill people, in the ways racism casts Black, Indigenous, and other people of color as defective. I slowly realized just how far the ideology of cure reaches.

I couldn't tell any one story without being interrupted by a half dozen others. I landed inside a knot of contradictions. Cure saves lives; cure manipulates lives; cure prioritizes some lives over others; cure makes profits; cure justifies violence; cure promises resolution to body-mind loss. I grappled through this tangle, picking up the same conundrums and questions repeatedly, turning them over and over, placing them side by side, creating patterns and dialogues.

I'm drawn back to the mosaic later in the day, the bright yellows now light browns in the afternoon shade. I stand again at the curb, admiring. At this angle, I see spirals and stars, concentric circles of blue, a river of deep red. I could swear they weren't here this morning.

I wrote prose poems, diatribes, provocations, personal stories. I delved into history. I crafted political analysis. Cure kept shifting. No single genre was able to contain all these fragments. For a long time, I couldn't envision this book's fractured wholeness.

And then, brilliant imperfection emerged, swirling between my words. I learned this idea in disability community from my longtime friend and fierce activist Sebastian Margaret. As a way of knowing, understanding, and living with disability and chronic illness, brilliant imperfection is rooted in the nonnegotiable value of body-mind difference. It resists the pressures of *normal* and *abnormal*. It defies the easy splitting of *natural* from *unnatural*. It has emerged from collective understandings and stubborn survivals. It is expressed in different ways by different communities. Sebastian taught it to me as an uppity, determined pride. Brilliant imperfection winds through this mosaic, a river of deep red.

Inside these shifting yellows, these ridges and bumps, these triangles and multisided oblongs, I'm still finding ideas, stories, and feelings that provoke me, surprise me, leave me wanting more.

Standing at the curb, I know that the spirals and stars, concentric circles of blue were here all along. They simply appeared because my angle changed.

Come sit with me. Let this mosaic that began in conversation spark a hundred new conversations.

A NOTE ON READING THIS BOOK:
THINKING ABOUT TRIGGER WARNINGS

i.

Some of the fragments in this book are razor sharp. The histories, ideas, realities I'm grappling with are full of pain and violence, grief and rage— involuntary sterilization, ritual abuse, suicide, centuries of colonialism, and bison massacre to name a few. These fragments might slice old wounds open, might remind us of scars long forgotten, might catapult us into past trauma. They might *trigger* us. I use that word intention- ally to reflect the abrupt, visceral tailspin some of us experience when encountering or being caught off guard by particular images or stories, smells or sounds, memories or emotions.[1]

In the late 1980s and 1990s, feminists developed the practice of trig- ger warnings to give people a heads-up before details of violence were spoken out loud. We weren't engaging in censorship or avoiding con- tentious issues, as some academics and activists claim today. Rather we knew that without trigger warnings many of us would lose access to conversations, communities, and learning spaces.

Applying these feminist lessons to this book has been tricky. I didn't know what to tag. Content that doesn't contain any triggers for one reader may hold many for another. None of us can reliably predict what will trig- ger someone we don't know well. While I believe warnings about explicit descriptions of violence are often helpful, that principle didn't provide me with clear guidance. These pages are a mosaic that places psychiatric hospitalization next to involuntary sterilization, resistance next to joy, community connection next to political thinking about hate language. Accounts of ableism, racism, classism, sexism, homophobia, transphobia, medicalization, and environmental destruction appear throughout the book. In other words, I could have tagged almost every piece here with a trigger warning. But that wouldn't help us know how and when to take care of ourselves and each other.

Trigger warnings are in essence tools for self-care and collective care. So let me remind readers that you can stop listening to or reading this book. You can read it fast or slow. You can read it out loud with your sister, partner, neighbor across the street. You can yell, type, breathe. Sign, sing, drink tea. Connect with your dog, cat, hamster, favorite tree. Call, text, Skype, Facebook, FaceTime with your friends. Lie in bed, roll, walk, dance, run. Woven through the book are prose poems about moments of brilliant imperfection in my life. Add your own moments to the mosaic. Do whatever works to ground yourself in the present.

ii.

Yet, after having asserted that tagging this book with specific trigger warnings would be difficult, if not impossible, I've done just that. Held within this feminist practice is an inherent tension. On the one hand, I can't possibly know and name all the potential triggers in the following pages, nor can I predict which stories, histories, and analyses will trigger what for whom. On the other hand, naming specific content that includes specific kinds of violence provides some of us with important, necessary, and, by definition, incomplete access. I want to let this tension exist without trying to resolve it.

What follows is a list of thirteen pieces that tell stories of sexual violence, ritual abuse, suicide, psychiatric hospitalization, and other kinds of institutionalization. None of the thirteen include gratuitous details or extended descriptions of violence.

"Defect"
"Personhood Is a Weapon"
"Cerebral Palsy"
"The Price of Diagnosis"
"Your Suicide Haunts Me"
"Carrie Buck I: Yearning"

"Carrie Buck II: Torrent of History"
"Carrie Buck III: Feebleminded"
"Lives Reduced to Case Files"
"Living with *Monkey*"
"Schizophrenia"
"Ashley's Father"
"Feeling Broken"

With all that said, welcome to this book, this mosaic, this grappling with cure.

WHITE PINES

In seventeenth- and eighteenth-century New England, the British Royal Navy claimed ownership of all the white pines over a hundred feet tall. English surveyors branded each trunk with three vertical hatchet marks, declaring it a crime for anyone but the king's representatives to cut these trees down. Broad and arrow straight, they became sailing ship masts, flexing in the wind as the Royal Navy sped around the world on its colonizing missions. By 1800, most of these big old trees were gone.

Now, two centuries later, I camp among white pines in occupied Abenaki Territory—known for the time being as Vermont—my favorite tent site at Ricker Pond strewn with needles. Neither as broad nor as tall as the mast trees, they still tower above the maple, beech, birch, balsam fir; sing in the wind, a deep-throated hush. Cones thud to the ground. Morning sun on the pond throws rippling shadows onto their bark. Crowns break and curve. Trunks split into three, four, five; grow bent around and through each other. They would never have been the king's trees.

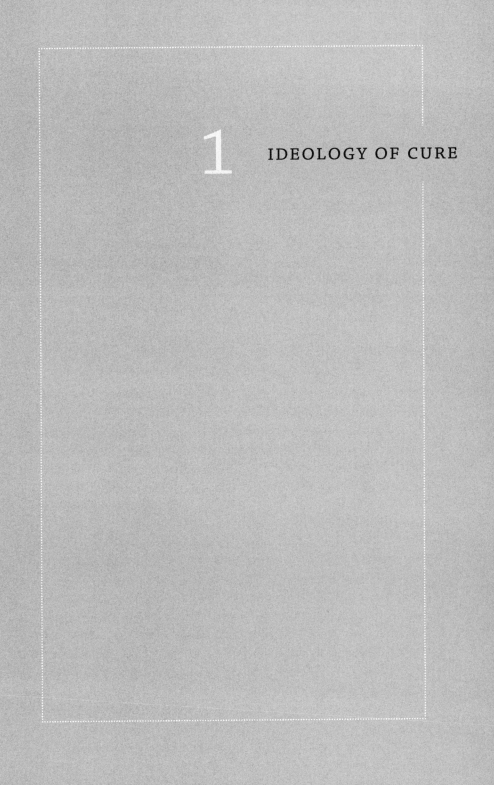

1   IDEOLOGY OF CURE

Birth

I am alive today because of medical technology. Otherwise my mother and I would have been dead long before my first breath, dead as the ovarian cyst that grew beside me. It was as big as a grapefruit before the doctors told her it had to be removed. Her grief, guilt, bitterness twined through that crisis called my birth. She was the first who wanted a cure for the havoc wreaked when the doctors pulled that cyst away. Did I experience it as twin, competitor, invader? Did we wrestle, embrace, vie for space?

They stole her ovary, and a week later I was born. If my father could have held me, I would have fit in one palm, nestled between fingertip and wrist, no bigger than a grapefruit myself, brain cells already dead and misfiring.

Anesthetic, IV, scalpels, sutures saved my mother and me, as did the surgeon who carefully lifted her right ovary out of her abdomen, leaving enough room for me to be born. And in turn, antibiotics, heat lamps, and an incubator kept me alive. I tell this story not as a tragedy, but a truth, a shrug of the shoulders, water over rock. Tell it neither grateful for that crisis nor bitter about the doctors who didn't inform my mother about the cyst growing inside her. They knew about it for years before my conception. Maybe I have them to thank for my birth, the luck of one sperm, one egg. My parents weren't salmon, thrashing a nest into gravel, laying eggs, flooding the water with spawn. But nonetheless, one egg, one sperm—conception is that fragile, that random.

At first all that mattered was her life and mine, but soon she started wishing for a cure, maybe even before she held me, skin to skin.

Prayers, Crystals, Vitamins

Strangers offer me Christian prayers or crystals and vitamins, always with the same intent—to touch me, fix me, mend my cerebral palsy, if only I will comply. They cry over me, wrap their arms around my shoulders, kiss my cheek. After five decades of these kinds of interactions, I still don't know how to rebuff their pity, how to tell them the simple truth that I'm not broken. Even if there were a cure for brain cells that died at birth, I'd refuse. I have no idea who I'd be without my tremoring and tense muscles, slurring tongue. They assume me unnatural, want to make me normal, take for granted the need and desire for cure.

Strangers ask me, "What's your defect?" To them, my body-mind just doesn't work right, defect being a variation of broken, supposedly neutral. But think of the things called defective—the MP3 player that won't turn on, the car that never ran reliably. They end up in the bottom drawer, dumpster, scrapyard. Defects are disposable and abnormal, body-minds or objects to eradicate.

Strangers pat me on the head. They whisper platitudes in my ear, clichés about courage and inspiration. They enthuse about how remarkable I am. They declare me special. Not long ago, a white woman, wearing dream-catcher earrings and a fringed leather tunic with a medicine wheel painted on its back, grabbed me in a bear hug. She told me that I, like all people who tremor, was a natural shaman. Yes, a shaman! In that split second, racism and ableism tumbled into each other yet again, the entitlement that leads white people to co-opt Indigenous spiritualities tangling into the ableist stereotypes that bestow disabled people with spiritual qualities. She whispered in my ear that if I were trained, I could become a great healer, directing me never to forget my specialness. Oh, how *special* disabled people are: we have *special* education, *special* needs, *special* spiritual abilities. That word drips condescension. It's no better than being defective.

Strangers, neighbors, and bullies have long called me *retard*. It doesn't happen so often now. Still, there's a guy down the road who, when he's drunk, taunts me as I walk by with my dog. But when I was a child, *retard* was a daily occurrence. Once, on a camping trip with my family, I joined a whole crowd of kids playing tag in and around the picnic shelter. A slow, clumsy nine-year-old, I quickly became "it." I chased and chased but caught no one. The game turned. Kids came close, ducked away, yelling *retard*. Frustrated, I yelled back for a while. *Retard* became *monkey*. My playmates circled me. Their words became a torrent. "You're a monkey. Monkey. Monkey." I gulped. I choked. I sobbed. Frustration, shame, humiliation swallowed me. My body-mind crumpled. It lasted two minutes or two hours—I don't know. When my father appeared, the circle scattered. Even as the word *monkey* connected me to the nonhuman natural world, I became supremely unnatural.

All these kids, adults, strangers join a legacy of naming disabled people not quite human. They approach me with prayers and vitamins, taunts and endless questions, convinced that I'm broken, special, an inspiration, a tragedy in need of cure, disposable—the momentum of centuries behind them. They have left me with sorrow, shame, and self-loathing.

Beliefs about Disability

Most nondisabled people believe that I need to be repaired. But in another time and place, they might have believed something different. Over the centuries in white Western culture, people now known as disabled have been monsters, gods, goddesses, and oracles. We have been proof of events that happened during our mothers' pregnancies, demonstrations of sin, and markers of evil. We have been evolutionary missing links, charity's favorite objects, the proving ground for Christian miracles. We have been the wild and exotic grist of freak shows, test subjects for the Nazis as they built and refined their gas chambers. We are burdens on society, useless eaters. We are tragedy and heroism. We are out-of-control, excessive, incapable. We are courage, metaphor, cautionary tale, downfall. We are better off dead. Some of these beliefs are long gone; others, still current. They migrate through the centuries, contradicting and bolstering each other.

Some days this history weighs my body-mind down. Depending on the time and place, priests, scientists, freak show managers, philosophers, charity workers, and doctors have all claimed to be the reigning experts on disability. Priests used to cast both disabled people and cure as the will of God. Scientists, naturalists, and anthropologists, responding to the theory of evolution, used to believe that disabled white people and people of color, both disabled and nondisabled, were the missing links between humans and primates. Freak show owners and managers used to make big profits by displaying those same groups of people as wondrous, savage, curious.

Philosophers and pundits have long blamed mothers for their disabled children. Two and three hundred years ago, according to conventional wisdom, a pregnant woman who saw an elephant might give birth to a child who had lumpy skin and enlarged limbs. Today when HIV-positive women, drug users, poor women surviving on welfare become pregnant, their choices are scrutinized and called immoral, particularly if their babies are born disabled. Sometimes these women are arrested, prosecuted, thrown in jail. Disabled or deaf parents-to-be who might pass on their congenital disabilities commonly face a barrage of criticism. When the deaf lesbian couple Sharon Duchesneau and Candace McCullough sought out a deaf man as a sperm donor so that their child would have a better chance of being deaf, the judgments flew. They were accused of being selfish and unfair to their unborn child. Over the centuries, deaf and disabled people have so often been considered immoral or the markers of immorality.

Charity has long organized itself around the twin notions that disability is tragic and disabled people are pitiful. We've become money-makers for Goodwill, the Salvation Army, the Muscular Dystrophy Association, Easter Seals, the Multiple Sclerosis Foundation, Autism Speaks, and on and on. In return they offer us sheltered employment for subminimum wages—sometimes as low as twenty-five cents an hour—and the promise of cure coming our way soon.

My joints ache in this cacophony of belief. For now, doctors inside the medical-industrial complex are the reigning experts, framing disability as a medical problem lodged in individual body-minds, which need to be treated or cured.

Overcoming Disability

Overcoming bombards disabled people. It's everywhere. I think of Whoopi Goldberg. In airports and along freeways, I see her plastered on a billboard sponsored by the Foundation for a Better Life (FBL).[1] Head in hands, dreadlocks threaded through fingers, she furrows her forehead in frustration. Or is it bemusement? She casts her eyes up, looking directly at her viewers. The tagline reads, "Overcaem dyslexia," coyly misspelling *overcame*. Underneath those two words brimming with stereotypes sits a red box containing the phrase "HARD WORK," and below that, the command "Pass It On."

The billboard makes me incredulous. The FBL tries to sell a pair of ideas: that Whoopi Goldberg—famous actor, hilarious comedian, Black woman—overcame learning disability through hard work, which, in turn, is a value we need to pass along. That disabled people can only succeed by overcoming disability is an ableist cliché, but let me turn it inside out. Maybe Goldberg became an actor exactly *because* of her dyslexia. Maybe she developed her kickass humor as a survival strategy to navigate the world as a Black, poor, disabled girl. Maybe she wouldn't have made it big without having a learning disability.

To portray dyslexia as a reversal of *m* and *e* in the word *overcame* is dismissive and stereotypical. To pose individual hard work, rather than broad-based disability access, as the key to success for people with dyslexia is absurd and ableist. To pair a Black woman with the value of hard work in a country that both names Black women as welfare queens and has, for centuries, exploited their back-breaking labor as maids and nannies, factory workers and field hands is demeaning and racist. Actually, the billboard enrages me.

....

Overcoming is a peculiar and puzzling concept. It means transcending, disavowing, rising above, conquering. Joy or grief *overcomes* us. An army *overcomes* its enemy. Whoopi Goldberg *overcomes* dyslexia.

I believe in success and failure, resistance and resilience. I've felt the weight of ableism, transphobia, and homophobia and witnessed the force of poverty and racism. I know about the refusal to give up and the trap of low expectations. I have a stake in access, interdependence, community, and fierceness mixed with luck and the hardest of work. I understand that survival sometimes depends on staying silent and hidden; other times, on claiming identity and pride. But overcoming mystifies me.

That concept requires dominating, subsuming, defeating something. Pairing disabled people with overcoming imagines disability as that thing. But how could I dominate my shaky hands, defeat my slurring tongue, even if I wanted to? How could Whoopi Goldberg subsume her dyslexia even as words waver and reverse on the page?

....

The chorus of a protest song echoes through my head: "Oh, deep in my heart / I do believe / We shall overcome / someday." This version of overcoming sung at Black civil rights protests and adopted by activists in a variety of social change movements since the 1960s means something different: collective action, transcending and dismantling white supremacy and poverty, believing in and working toward a future of liberation. But what this song doesn't mean is equally telling. It doesn't urge people into a future without, beyond, or in spite of Blackness. Without making an analogy between racism and ableism, the civil rights movement and disability politics, I want to note the striking contrast between "We Shall Overcome" and the FBL's "Overcaem dyslexia." The first grapples with systems of oppression; the second, with individualized body-mind conditions.

Sometimes disabled people overcome specific moments of ableism— we exceed low expectations, problem-solve lack of access, avoid nursing homes or long-term psych facilities, narrowly escape police brutality and prison. However, I'm not sure that overcoming *disability* itself is an actual possibility for most of us. Yet in a world that places extraordinary value in cure, the belief that we can defeat or transcend body-mind conditions through individual hard work is convenient. Overcoming is cure's backup plan.

Hope in Motion

Cure is inextricably linked to hope. I'm remembering a documentary called *Christopher Reeve: Hope in Motion* about the late, famed actor who became a quadriplegic in a horse-riding accident.[2] As a self-appointed spokesman for cure, Reeve repeatedly expressed this link, never failing to make me angry. In the film, he brashly dismisses disabled people who question the notion of cure, saying, "There are some people who just really don't dare to hope."

I'll be blunt: *Christopher Reeve: Hope in Motion* strikes me as propaganda. The narrator uses the words *overcome, fight, determination, inspirational, unwavering will, working tirelessly, amazing results* more times than I care to count. As these words pile one on top of another accompanied by rising violin music, the film reveals itself as another over-the-top story about a tragically disabled man who beats the odds, overcomes his paralysis, and through his courageous struggle gives us hope and inspiration. There is nothing unusual here, just the same old stereotypes.

The camera follows Reeve as he works out, grinding through his daily physical therapy routines, swimming in rehab pools, elated by his occasional water-assisted step. He grimaces, laboring, flashing quick smiles of triumph, always surrounded by a team of therapists, nurses, and aides.

The camera follows him as he chooses experimental surgery to implant a pacemaker in his abdomen with the hope that he might be able to breathe without a ventilator. His surgeon, Raymond Onders, says, "Our goal is to allow a patient to breathe the way he was born to breathe, to breathe more normally through the use of his own diaphragm." His words epitomize cure rhetoric, medical intervention returning body-minds deemed abnormal to their natural states of being, judging one piece of technology more normal than another. Relentlessly Reeve prepares for cure.

For a moment, I let go of my anger. *Christopher, what did you miss the most? Gripping a horse between your knees, feeling her supple muscles move against your legs, following and directing her rhythm with that wordless language of shifting weight and pressure? Walking on a set, a particular turn of hip and shoulder cuing the next line? Cavorting with your children and wife away from the camera?* I imagine his loss as deep as his drive for a cure.

The camera follows him around the globe as he advocates, lobbies, and fund-raises for stem cell research and a cure for spinal cord injuries. Repeatedly he enlists the rhetoric of hope and conquering diseases, leveraging pity and tragedy to make his case. *Christopher, how often did strangers pat your head? Did their pity ever exhaust you?*

....

His story is as much about wealth, whiteness, and male privilege, about great and infuriating entitlement, as it is about disability. He claims that "the most disabling thing about being disabled is a feeling of hopelessness." He means despair about his ongoing paralysis, not the ableist violence, isolation, poverty, and lack of education and employment faced by many disabled people. He says on the eighth anniversary of his accident: "I was forty-two when I was injured, and now I'm fifty. How long is it really going to be until human trials? Will they happen here, or will I have to go overseas? I don't want to be a senior citizen when I'm cured. To get up, only to crawl around in my old age." Only a wealthy white man with a beautiful white woman at his side could possess this much entitlement. Yet, not far beneath his words, I hear the fear of body-mind change, aging, and death.

Halfway through the documentary, Reeve surprises me. He sits in a rehab room surrounded by medical machinery, focusing hard as he learns to breathe with his new pacemaker, working to time his inhale to the pulse of this little electrical box. The narrator tells us that for eight vent-using years Reeve had no sense of smell, her tone meant to evoke pity and sympathy, to confirm his obvious pursuit of hope through cure. Breathing without his vent, he asks for a smell challenge. After he closes his eyes, a woman tips an open can of Folgers ground coffee under his nose. As violin music rises in the background, he identifies coffee, a smile emerging on his face. Then an orange, skin broken open, and finally chocolate mint. Of course, the film is telling that oh-so-familiar story, a story told thousands of times—the disabled person miraculously recovering, learning to walk, talk, see, hear, or, in this case, smell again. It reaffirms the tragedy of disability, the need for cure. At the same time, something compels me to pay closer attention as Reeve relishes those familiar scents. He says, "I don't think at the beginning of my injury that I would have ever realized how much one thing would matter, the ability to smell, the ability to eat. . . . I was looking at the big picture—what's the quickest research that's going to get me up and back on a horse. . . . But the little changes . . . to be able to smell, I'm surprised by how satisfying those little discoveries are." In this moment he isn't renouncing cure and its link to hope, but he is grappling with the nuances of body-mind loss.

Christopher, you were a privileged, wealthy, lucky disabled person. That is until your luck ran out, and you died of an out-of-control infection. In the end, I wish you could have found hope through your disabled body-mind, through community, through a desire for social justice. Instead ableism intertwined with your great sense of entitlement and made cure irresistible.

Rebelling against Cure

Over the years, I have ranted repeatedly about cure and the medicalization of disabled people. For decades, disability activists have been saying, "Leave our body-minds alone. Stop justifying and explaining your oppressive crap by measuring, comparing, judging, and creating theories about us." Declaring disability a matter of social justice is an important act of resistance—disability residing not in paralysis but in stairs without an accompanying ramp, not in blindness but in the lack of braille and audio books, not in dyslexia but in teaching methods unwilling to flex. In this declaration, disability politics joins other social change movements in the ongoing work of locating the problems of injustice not in individual body-minds but in the world.

Christopher Reeve has frequented my rants. As a rich, white man with a whole lot of access to the media and lawmakers, we needed him to advocate for social justice. He could have talked about education, unemployment, and disability access, about Medicaid funding for community-based living and the problem of warehousing disabled people in nursing homes, about stereotypes and lies, about violence, police brutality, isolation, and poverty. But he didn't.

At the same time, my ranting neither begins nor ends with Reeve. In his quest for cure, he followed the lead of many disability charity organizations that use a fraction of their money to build ramps, buy wheelchairs, revamp schools. They're not funding an end to ableism. Rather they're raising money for research and cure. They shamelessly use pity, tragedy, and the belief that we would all be better off without disability.

To escape this quagmire—pity curling into violence, charity laced with the impulse to do away with disability—many of us have chosen rebellion. I for one have honed the blunt art of ranting.

....

One day in my work as an activist-writer, I'm at a podium, debunking lies about disability and cure, ranting yet again about Reeve. I pause, look at the audience, and see my friend P. standing at the back of the room. Her story of surviving cancer—surgery, chemo, radiation, her brush with death—flashes through me. All at once, my words feel like empty rhetoric. I have no idea what cure means to her.

Later I go to dinner with her and a half dozen other people to continue the conversation. I don't know what to expect. I feel nervous, not quite ready. Over food, our talk turns to story. My friend P. tells us how she's been encouraged in dozens of ways to think about her life with cancer as a battle. She says, "I'm not at war with my body, but at the same time, I won't passively let my cancerous cells have their way with me." We talk about healing and recovery, surviving and dying. No one invokes hope or overcoming. I sit here listening. For now, my impulse to rant has vanished.

The Restoration of Health

As an ideology seeped into every corner of white Western thought and culture, cure rides on the back of *normal* and *natural*. Insidious and pervasive, it impacts most of us. In response, we need neither a wholehearted acceptance nor an outright rejection of cure, but rather a broadbased grappling.

The American Heritage Dictionary defines cure as the "restoration of health." Those three words seem simple enough, but actually *health* is a mire. Today inside white Western medicine, health ranges from individual and communal body-mind comfort to profound social control. Between these two poles, a multitude of practices exist. Health promotes both the well-being sustained by good food and the products sold by the multimillion-dollar diet industry. Health endorses both effective pain management for folks who live with chronic pain and the policed refusal to prescribe narcotic-based pain relief to people perceived as drugseeking. Health both saves lives and aggressively markets synthetic growth hormones to children whose only body-mind "problem" is being short.

Amidst these contradictions, I could try to determine who's healthy and who's not, acting as if there might be a single objective standard. I could struggle to clarify the relationship between health and disability. I could work, as many activists and healers do, to redefine health, moving toward theories and practices that contribute to the well-being of entire communities. But in using the *American Heritage Dictionary* definition as a springboard, I actually want to move away from this mire altogether and follow the word *restoration*.

....

To restore a house that's falling down or a tallgrass prairie ecosystem that's been devastated is to return it to an earlier, and often better, condition. In this return, we try to undo the damage, wishing the damage had never happened. Talk to anyone who does restoration work—carpenters who rebuild 150-year-old neglected houses or conservation biologists who turn agribusiness cornfields back to tallgrass prairie—and they'll say it's a complex undertaking. A fluid, responsive process, restoration requires digging into the past, stretching toward the future, working hard in the present. And the end results rarely, if ever, match the original state.[3]

Restoring a tallgrass prairie means rebuilding a dynamic system that has been destroyed by the near extinction of bison, the presence of cattle, and generations of agribusiness farming and fire suppression. The goal isn't to re-create a static landscape somehow frozen in time, but rather to foster dynamic interdependencies, ranging from clods of dirt to towering thunderheads, tiny microbes to herds of bison. This work builds on knowledge about and experience with an eight-thousand-year-old ecosystem, of which only remnants remain—isolated pockets of leadplants, milkweed, burr oaks, and switchgrass growing in cemeteries and on remote bluffs, somehow miraculously surviving. The intention is to mirror this historical ecosystem as closely as possible, even though some element is bound to be missing or different, the return close but not complete.

The process of restoration is simpler with a static object—an antique chair or old house. Still, if the carpenters aren't using axe-hewn timbers of assorted and quirky sizes, mixing the plaster with horse hair, building at least a few walls with chicken wire, using newspaper, rags, or nothing at all for insulation, then the return will be incomplete. It will be possibly sturdier and definitely more energy efficient, but different from the original house.

....

I circle back to the ideology of cure. Framing it as a kind of restoration reveals the most obvious and essential tenets. First, cure requires damage, locating the harm entirely within individual human body-minds, operating as if each person were their own ecosystem. Second, it grounds itself in an original state of being, relying on a belief that what existed before is superior to what exists currently. And finally, it seeks to return what is damaged to that former state of being.

But for some of us, even if we accept disability as damage to individual body-minds, these tenets quickly become tangled, because an original nondisabled state of being doesn't exist. How would I, or the medical-industrial complex, go about restoring my body-mind? The vision of me without tremoring hands and slurred speech, with more balance and coordination doesn't originate from my visceral history. Rather it arises from an imagination of what I should be like, from some definition of *normal* and *natural*.

Walking in the Prairie

My friend J. and I walk in the summer rain through a thirty-acre pocket of tallgrass prairie that was not so long ago one big agribusiness cornfield. We follow the path mowed as a firebreak. He carries a big, flowered umbrella. Water droplets hang on the grasses. Spider webs glint. The bee balm hasn't blossomed yet. He points out the numerous patches of birch, goldenrod, and thistle. The first two belong here but need to be thinned out. The thistle, on the other hand, should be entirely uprooted. The Canada wild rye waves, the big bluestem almost open. Clusters of sunflowers brighten the rainy day. We pause to admire the cornflowers and asters. The songbirds and butterflies have taken shelter. For the moment, all is quiet. Soon my jeans are sopping wet from the knees down. This little piece of prairie is utterly different from a cornfield.

A whole group of people, including J., worked for over a decade to restore this land. With financial and material help from Wisconsin's Department of Natural Resources, they mowed and burned the cornfield. They broadcast the seed—sack upon sack of the right mix that might replicate the tallgrass prairie that was once here. They rooted out thistle and prickly ash. They saved money for more seed, working to undo the two centuries of environmental destruction wreaked by plows, pesticides, acres upon acres of soybeans and corn.

The Department of Natural Resources partners with this work precisely because the damage is so great. Without the massive web of prairie roots to anchor the earth, the land now known as Wisconsin is literally draining away. Rain catches the topsoil, washing it from field to creek to river to ocean. Prairie restoration reverses this process, both stabilizing and creating soil. J. and his friends worked hard, remembering all the while that neither they nor the dairy farmer down the road owned this land. It was stolen a century and a half ago from the eastern Dakota people. The histories of grass, dirt, bison massacre, genocide live here, floating in the air, tunneled into the earth.

During my visits to see J., I have taken this walk a dozen times over the last fifteen years—at noon with the sun blazing, at dusk with fireflies lacing the grasses, at dawn with finches and warblers greeting the day. My feet still feel the old cornfield furrows.

As we return to the farmhouse, I think about *natural* and *unnatural*, trying to grasp their meanings. Is an agribusiness cornfield unnatural, a
restored prairie natural? How about the abundance of thistle, absence
of bison, those old corn furrows? What was once normal here; what can
we consider normal now?

    Or are these the wrong questions? Maybe the earth just holds layer
upon layer of history.

TWITCHES AND TREMORS

You and I have just finished facilitating a day-long training.
Back in our hotel room, we collapse onto a bed, out of
words, breath, energy. We lie next to each other, your head
light against my shoulder. You brush my ribs. I flinch.
Your hands twitch, twitch again, on my skin. I answer with
tremor, starting as always behind my right shoulder blade,
descending my arm. My touch vibrates into you. Your hands
twitch and curl over me, triggering a cascade of tremors.
Slow, slow—my muscles don't lock. Tremors rise to meet
twitches, call and response.

I've had lovers tell me how good my shaky touch feels,
tremors likened to extra caresses or driving over a gravel
road, their words an antidote to shame. But until now, I had
never felt the pleasure they describe. Your twitches spread
across my skin—tingle, echo, dance.

2   VIOLENCE OF CURE

Defect

Defectiveness justifies cure and makes it essential. Across the centuries, how many communities have been declared inherently defective by white people, rich people, nondisabled people, men backed by medical, scientific, academic, and state authority? I ask this question rather than answer it, because any list I create will be incomplete. White women suffragists fighting for the right to vote were declared defective as a way of undercutting their demands. Black people kidnapped from Africa and enslaved in the Americas were declared defective as a way to justify and strengthen the institution of slavery. Immigrants at Ellis Island were declared defective and refused entry to the United States. Lesbians and gay men were declared defective and given hormones and shock treatments to cure their sexual desires. And today, police shoot homeless people, juries and judges sentence intellectually disabled Black men to death row, schools track Indigenous, Black, Latinx, poor, and disabled children into special ed—all of them deemed defective in one way or another. The list of peoples keeps growing, the damage deepening.[1]

Defectiveness wields incredible power because ableism builds and maintains the notion that defective body-minds are undesirable, worthless, disposable, or in need of cure. In a world without ableism, *defective*, meaning the "imperfection of a bodily system," would probably not even exist. But if it did, it would only be a neutral descriptor. However, in today's world where ableism fundamentally shapes white Western cultural definitions of normal and abnormal, worthy and unworthy, whole and broken body-minds, any person or community named defective can be targeted without question or hesitation for eradication, imprisonment, institutionalization. The ableist invention of defectiveness functions as an indisputable justification not only for cure but also for many systems of oppression.

....

Defective arcs repeatedly through history. Let me trace a single trajectory, starting in 1851, though I could begin nearly anywhere. Dr. Samuel Cartwright wrote in the *New Orleans Medical and Surgical Journal*: "It is this *defective* hematosis, or atmospherization of the blood, conjoined with a deficiency of cerebral matter in the cranium . . . which has rendered the people of Africa unable to take care of themselves" (emphasis added).[2] Using scientific language, Cartwright defended and justified slavery, casting Black people as inferior and racist stereotypes as medical truth. Defectiveness and deficiency lay at the center of his argument.

In the same article, he coined several "diseases of the mind": *drapetomania*, which he claimed led enslaved African Americans to run away, and *dysaesthesia aethiopica*, which led them to be lazy. These diagnoses not only turned Black resistance into illness but also allowed Cartwright to frame white power and control as cure: "The complaint [of *dysaesthesia aethiopica*] is easily curable. . . . The best means . . . is, first, to have the patient well washed with warm water and soap; then, to anoint it all over in oil, and to slap the oil in with a broad leather strap."[3] Cartwright's sleight of hand is brutal. Enslaved Black people become patients and "it." The violence they endured becomes cure. The disabling nature of slavery is hidden away. Cartwright revealed in no uncertain terms the social control embedded in the declaration of defectiveness.

His words travel from 1851 to 1968, landing with white psychiatrists Walter Bromberg and Frank Simon, who pontificated: "The stress of asserting civil rights in the United States these past ten years and the corresponding nationalistic fervor of Afro-American nations . . . has stimulated specific reactive psychoses in American Negroes."[4] Cartwright's claims transform and yet stay the same, the 1851 "defective hematosis" twisting into the 1968 "specific reactive psychoses." Bromberg and Simon continued, "The particular symptomology we have observed, for which the term 'protest psychosis' is suggested, is influenced by . . . the Civil Rights Movement . . . and is colored by a denial of Caucasian values. . . . This protest psychosis among prisoners is virtually a repudiation of 'white civilization.'"[5] In coining this new diagnosis "protest psychosis," cousin to schizophrenia, and declaring it widespread among Blacks who defied white supremacy, they, like Cartwright, framed resistance as pathology. They used defectiveness yet again to justify violence—this time the locking up of Black men in prisons and psychiatric facilities and drugging them with antipsychotic meds.

Bromberg and Simon's words travel from 1968 to 2014, landing in the grand jury testimony of the white police officer, Darren Wilson, who shot and killed the young, Black, unarmed Michael Brown in Ferguson, Missouri. In his testimony, Wilson recounts the altercation that happened moments before the shooting: "When I grabbed him, . . . I felt like a five-year-old holding onto Hulk Hogan [a six-foot-seven, three-hundred-pound professional wrestler]. . . . That's how big he felt and how small I felt."[6] There's no reflection of an adult man and a teenager of almost equal size—both of them six foot four, Brown weighing more and Wilson, the adult, armed and wielding the power of the state. Instead, Wilson creates a picture of a monstrously overpowering Black man. He continues, claiming at one point that the eighteen-year-old "had the most intense aggressive face. The only way I can describe it, it looks like a *demon*" (emphasis added). Wilson remembers that once he started shooting, Brown was "still coming at me, he hadn't slowed down. . . . It looked like he was almost bulking up to run through the shots." Brown becomes in Wilson's story a monster, an embodiment of evil, a superhuman impervious to bullets.[7]

Unlike Cartwright, Bromberg, and Simon, Wilson doesn't characterize all Black people, wield diagnosis, or directly call Brown defective. Yet in painting him as an overpowering superhuman demon, Wilson calls on centuries of racism, his testimony joining with *drapetomania*, *dysaesthesia aethiopica*, and *protest psychosis*.

Cartwright and the rest use the ableist invention of defectiveness in order to explain and justify the practices of enslavement, imprisonment, institutionalization, and state violence. In essence, they fortify white supremacy by leveraging ableism.

. . . .

Entire body-minds, communities, cultures are squeezed into *defective*. And then that single blunt concept turns, becoming *defect*. Bullies hurl it as an insult. Strangers ask it out of curiosity. Doctors note it in medical files. Judges and juries hear it in testimony. Scientists study it as truth. Politicians write it into policy. *Defect* and *defective* explode with hate, power, and control.

At the Center of Cure Lies Eradication

I play out an imaginary future in my head: disability has been cured. The medical-industrial complex has worked toward this moment for many decades. The visceral experiences named by thousands of diagnostic labels will soon cease to exist both in individual body-minds and collectively in the world. I think about myself and all the disabled people around me—acquaintances, friends, coworkers, neighbors, family members, lovers, activists, cultural workers. I think about what we offer the world—comedy, poetry, performance art, passionate activism, sexy films, important thinking, good conversation, fun. I think about who we are and the ways in which our particular body-minds have shaped us. Who would we be without disability?

Disability activist Harriet McBryde Johnson writes, "Are [disabled people] 'worse off'? I don't think so. Not in any meaningful sense. There are too many variables. For those of us with congenital conditions, disability shapes all we are. Those disabled later in life adapt. We take constraints that no one would choose and build rich and satisfying lives within them. We enjoy pleasures other people enjoy, and pleasures peculiarly our own. We have something the world needs."[8] In my imaginary future, we, or future generations like us, wouldn't exist. I feel neither triumph nor progress but loss.

....

At the center of cure lies eradication and the many kinds of violence that accompany it. On the surface, this claim appears hyperbolic. Many lives, including my own, depend on or have been made possible by cure and its technologies. As it supports and extends life, the restoration of health seems to be the opposite of eradication. But cure arrives in many different guises, connected to elimination and erasure in a variety of configurations.

In one permutation, the same medical-industrial complex that saved my mother and me would, if it could, eliminate cerebral palsy from both my individual body-mind and the world at large. In this guise, a multitude of visceral differences would cease to exist. They include both life-threatening conditions (AIDS, malaria, smallpox, and many kinds of cancer, to name a few) and conditions deemed defects but that aren't necessarily lethal (autism, cerebral palsy, hearing voices, and the lasting impacts of spinal cord injuries, for example). The list of body-mind differences, illnesses, and so-called defects that the medical-industrial complex wants to eradicate goes on and on. This kind of elimination benefits some of us in significant ways—saving our lives or increasing our comfort. At the same time, it also commits damage, routinely turning body-minds into medical objects and creating lies about *normal* and *natural*.

In a second permutation, the medical-industrial complex focuses not on specific diseases and disorders but rather on the people who have these conditions. This kind of eradication is often intent on changing the future by manipulating the present. I think about disability-selective abortion. In today's world, the ideology of cure doesn't suggest that we round up everyone who has Down syndrome and eliminate them. Instead, genetic testing and counseling are paired with abortion, setting the scene for eradicating the future possibility of people with Down.

Every day doctors pressure pregnant people to undergo genetic testing, and counselors release the results and guide the course of the conversations that follow. As a result, prospective parents in the United States decide to abort about two-thirds of fetuses predicted to have Down.[9] This termination of pregnancy for the specific reason of not wanting a disabled child clearly manipulates the present. Eradication happens in this moment, but it also extends into a future that is no more than nine months away. In that future, one less person with Down syndrome exists. The choice of each individual parent stacks up until thousands of fetuses predicted to have Down are aborted every year. I'm less interested in the rightness or wrongness of these choices by themselves than in the distinct pattern they create when placed side by side, exposing the systemic desire to erase a whole group of people. This future-focused eradication is easy to shrug past, because many of us have been seduced into believing the need to eliminate disability and "defectiveness" is intuitively obvious.

In a third permutation, the resolve to eradicate particular body-mind conditions stops for nothing, including the possibility of death in the present. I think about the separation of conjoined twins. These surgeries are intensely risky and not always necessary for survival and well-being. Often the high-tech, hours-long medical procedures become media spectacles, with cameras following the families and filming the operations. In an ABC News story from 2015 about the separation of the infants Connor and Carter Mirabal, a nurse says, "Now they are truly boys, individuals," suggesting that a non-conjoined body-mind is a requirement for individuality, possibly even for personhood. Moments later one of the surgeons echoes her sentiments: "It felt good to see them in separate rooms. They seem like individuals now."[10] This emphasis on individuality underlines their belief in the superiority of one kind of body-mind over another. We never learn how Connor and Carter were actually doing before. Was this surgery essential for their survival? Or was it an exercise in eliminating what is deemed abnormal and defective, reshaping it to be normal?

In some separation surgeries, doctors intentionally sacrifice one of the twins in order to save the other, most often when neither will survive if they remain conjoined. This exact situation landed in the court system in the United Kingdom in 2000. Doctors at St. Mary's Hospital in Manchester, England, wanted to pursue the separation of Gracie and Rosie Attard, a surgery that they knew would lead to Rosie's death. Their parents, Michaelangelo and Rina Attard, refused to give consent. The surgeons sued the Attards and won. In the legal decision, the judges' logic is revealing. One declared, "The operation would give [Rosie], even in death, bodily integrity as a human being."[11] Without apology, he justified the eradication of this disabled girl through an argument about personhood. In his logic, literal elimination of life becomes cure.

....

In all three configurations, elimination of some kind—of a disease, of future existence, of present-day embodiments, of life itself—is essential to the work of cure. Sometimes these eradications result in benefit, but they can also cause individual death and the diminishment of whole groups of people. The violence that shadows these erasures could be framed as a mere side effect, or the unavoidable cost, of saving lives and normalizing body-minds.

But let me suggest a different framing: that this violence is something more inherent—a consequence, an impact, even an intent. I don't mean that each individual instance of cure is violent. Remember, the restoration of health arrives in many slippery guises. Rather I mean that as a widespread ideology centered on eradication, cure always operates in relationship to violence.

Personhood Is a Weapon

Some of us are granted personhood as our birthright, but others are required to prove and defend it every day. And when we fail this perverse test, we're in trouble. Listen. I want us to remember Terri Schiavo. Debates about her raged in the news in 2004 and 2005.[12]

Whatever happens after we die, our body-minds composting back to earth and air, I hope it's more peaceful than Terri Schiavo's last few days as she died of dehydration. Everyone—her parents, her husband, her doctors, the media—had an opinion about her and the feeding tube that had just been removed from her stomach.

She was a white woman who collapsed one day, her body-mind changing radically in a matter of minutes as oxygen stopped flowing to her brain and then started again. Some say she lost her ability to communicate, to think, to feel. Or perhaps we lost our capacity to listen. We'll never know what floated beneath her skin. I want us to mourn for her.

Pundits and reporters, activists and scholars have written about her endlessly. I don't know why I'm adding to their pile of words, except my memory of her won't leave me alone.

She was a heterosexual woman whose husband decided she'd rather die than be disabled. Her hands curled, stiffened, joints freezing into contraction. He asserted his patriarchal ownership, refusing to let nurses slide rolled towels into her hands to help loosen her muscles. Nor would he allow them to teach her to swallow again, even though there was every sign that she could. He spent all his court-awarded settlement money on lawyers rather than care, comfort, and assistive technology. What words or fluttering images did she hold in her muscles and bones?

So many people surrounding Terri Schiavo assumed that she knew and felt nothing. Over and over again neurologists, journalists, judges made decisions about her body-mind based on the beliefs that language and self-awareness make us worthy, that death is better than disability, that withdrawing the basic human rights of food and water can be acts of compassion.

I could ponder self-consciousness, spiritual connection, and the divide between human and nonhuman. I could argue with the bioethicists who separate humanness from personhood, declaring pigs and chimpanzees to have more value than infants and significantly disabled people. But really, I'm not interested. I want us to rage for her.

She was a woman living in a hospital bed, referred to as a vegetable more than once. Did she lie in a river of shadow and light, pressure and sound? That too, we will never know. When she died, did we call her name?

Body-minds have value. Certainly I mean our own human selves, but

I also mean heron, firefly, weeping willow. I mean dragonfly, birch, barn swallow. I mean goat and bantam rooster, mosquito and wood frog, fox and vulture—the multitude of beings that make home on this planet. I mean all body-minds, regardless of personhood.

She appeared to track the motion of balloons across her hospital room and grinned lopsidedly into the camera. Her life hung between a husband who said one thing and parents who said another, between legal pronouncements and diagnostic judgments. Do we remember her? I don't mean the editorials, the pro-life versus pro-choice rhetoric, the religious and secular arguments, the political protest and vigil staged outside her hospice, the last-minute drama as Florida's governor Jeb Bush and the U.S. Congress tried to intervene. I mean: do we remember her?

Too many of us acted as if Terri Schiavo's body-mind stopped being her own. Depending on who we were and what stake we had in her life or death, we projected our fear, belief, hope, disgust, love, certainty onto her.

I'm trying to say that life and death sometimes hangs on an acknowledgement of personhood. Trying to say that personhood is used all too often as a weapon. Trying to say that while personhood holds tremendous power, its definitions are always arbitrary. Trying to say—I stutter over the gravity of those words.

Great Turmoil

....

In the 1950s we used pigs at the Nevada Test Site to study the impact of radiation on humans, their skin resembling our own.

> Remember the extinct
> passenger pigeon, Carolina parakeet,
> ivory-billed woodpecker. They became
> meat, plumes, collector items.

I feel.

Since the 1940s we've turned the eyes of rabbits into open sores as we develop cosmetics.

> Remember the air full
> of toxins, the water turned
> to sludge, the wildfires
> and floods.

I feel great turmoil.

Today we research the mucus that lines the lungs of elephant seals as a potential treatment, even cure, for cystic fibrosis.

> Remember the rivers
> that no longer run
> to the ocean, the great expanses
> of forest now barren.

I feel great turmoil about being human.

We treat so many body-minds as if they matter only in service to our own.

> Remember the dams we've built,
> the prairies we've plowed under,
> the oil wells we've drilled.

Any reckoning with personhood has to account for this destruction too.

MAPLES

My most constant writing companions are a pair of big,
old maples filling the second-story window near my desk.
Currently leafed out, a luscious green, the trees worry me.
A year ago the power company not so carefully trimmed
branches away from the electric lines, and this summer I'm
noticing dead twigs amidst their greenery. Three months
from now, they will begin to shed leaves, becoming an
orange-yellow luminescence on clear fall days, by November
revealing the bare bones of their trunks and branches.
Five months after that, leaves will emerge, pale-green fists
unfurling themselves as the days lengthen and the nights
rise above freezing. I've known them for over a decade, an
intimate, wordless relationship.

3 IN TANDEM WITH CURE

Cerebral Palsy

I remember being twelve years old, my parents bringing me to the Crippled Children's Division (CCD) at the University of Oregon for yet another round of diagnostic testing. I remember walking back and forth for an orthopedist, stacking blocks for a physical therapist, and solving puzzles for a team of psychologists. I knew this diagnostic routine all too well. I can't count how many IQ tests I took, how many soundproof rooms I sat in as audiologists checked my hearing, how many words I repeated, one after another, as speech pathologists analyzed which sounds my tongue stumbled over. All the orthopedists, physical therapists, psychologists, audiologists, speech pathologists blur together. I can't remember a single face, but the one-way mirrors—those glass walls behind which they watched my every move—remain vivid.

At CCD, after two days of testing, the physical therapist sat us down and told my parents that I had cerebral palsy. Years later I learned she was the first medical provider to give me that diagnosis. It crushed my parents, who had brought me there specifically to find a cure. Instead we returned home with a diagnosis for an incurable condition and my first orthopedic equipment since the big blocky shoes that helped me learn to walk.

I never believed in cure exactly, even as I yearned to be nondisabled. But I did want to know what happened between my brain and my tremoring hands, slurring tongue, stumbling feet—an explanation beyond the story of brain cells dying. The physical therapists and orthopedists never gave me a satisfactory answer. I imagined electrical storms and collapsing bridges, a twelve-year-old turning my body-mind into a metaphor, out-of-control and broken. I didn't liken my tremors to sunlight stuttering through wind-tossed trees, my slurs to an earthworm curling over itself, my stumbles to the erratic rhythm of a pileated woodpecker drumming a tree.

....

I struggled with the orthopedic equipment we brought home. I strapped three-pound cuffs to my forearms. Supposedly they made it harder for me to shake, training my muscles not to tremor. My arms sweated and ached under the weight. When I wasn't using the cuffs, I buckled magnets to my wrists, clamped my arms to a metal board positioned on the kitchen table, and tried the task of writing, tremors restrained. The magnets were a dismal failure, but the cuffs I wore through eighth grade, hating them more every day. I could bear the physical discomfort but not the shame—those leather-covered lead weights revealing my cerebral palsy in yet another way. My mother and I fought; she won, trading her dreams of cure for faith in treatment.

Eventually I refused to strap the weights onto my shakier right arm; it hurt too much. Then I lost the left cuff, relieved. In contrast, I never stopped using the electric typewriter we acquired through CCD. Once my mother abandoned her hopes of teaching me to touch-type, I learned an efficient two-fingered peck, using eraser-tipped pencils, still slow but much faster than my longhand ever was. I wore out two typewriters before I bought my first computer. Adaptation carries far more appeal than treatment.

....

I ride slow loops of memory, each faint arc shimmering, back and back to where diagnosis started. A physical therapist says the words *cerebral palsy*. An orthopedist suggests heel cord surgery. Reflections in a shiny one-way mirror stare at me. A speech therapist reaches into my mouth to hold, encourage, shape the muscle of my tongue. Memory glimmers— another earlier physical therapy office. And here, here: my first flash— white coats, voices, a table, fear of falling. I look up.

It's 1966, and I am two and a half years old, no longer stumping around on my knees but balancing on my own two feet, taking my first shaky steps—a loop of its own with no trace of memory. I'm not talking yet, not a single spoken word. I use a rudimentary sign language of my own creation.

It's 1966, and my parents have brought me to this institution, which at its founding in 1908 was known as the State Institution for the Feeble-Minded, thirty years later was renamed the Oregon Fairview Home, and by the time I show up is called the Fairview Hospital and Training Center. Historians Philip Ferguson, Diane Ferguson, and Meredith Brodsky write, "Fairview Training Center . . . was not the first such institution to open or the last to close. Even at its peak population, it was not the biggest. As those who lived there know only too well, it definitely was not the best, but as others who lived elsewhere can also testify, it certainly was not the worst. . . . If there can be such a thing, the Fairview Training Center could be called a 'typical' institution for people with developmental disabilities."[1]

It's 1966, and the doctors give me an IQ test. Fifty years earlier, American eugenicist Henry Goddard sought a way to quantify intelligence, eager to have a tool that would reveal the feeblemindedness he and many others believed was overtaking the United States. To this end, he translated, revised, and championed a French intelligence test. He coined the word *moron*. He put his work through trial runs at Ellis Island using Jewish, Hungarian, Russian, and Italian immigrants as his subjects. He found 40 percent of the people he tested to be morons, which of course was the whole point—to prove what eugenicists already believed about immigrants and feeblemindedness.[2] Goddard's work became the test I take.

It's 1966, and Fairview houses nearly three thousand people. In 1920 we were called idiot, imbecile, and moron; in 1950, retarded and handicapped; and now we are beginning to be named developmentally disabled, not yet known as intellectually disabled. The diagnostic language slips and slides over the decades. Of the three thousand people who live here, many have been locked away for their entire lives.

It's 1966, and I score badly on their tests. Not many years before, they would have declared me a *low grade moron* or a *high grade imbecile*, but by the 1960s the words have changed, even as the laws and institutions have not. I become *mentally retarded*.

It's 1966, and Oregon doctors still sterilize people on a monthly basis. They use the state's eugenics legislation, first passed in 1917, to authorize involuntary castrations, vasectomies, hysterectomies, and tubal ligations. Before the law is repealed in 1983, they perform at least 2,648 of these surgeries.[3]

It's 1966, and I join the ranks of those targeted. The Oregon law names us "feeble-minded, insane, epileptics, habitual criminals, moral degenerates, and sexual perverts, who are persons potential to producing offspring who, because of inheritance of inferior or antisocial traits, would probably become a social menace."[4] Sterilization is often the sole criteria for release from Fairview.

If my parents did nothing else, they didn't leave me there. They definitely could have.

Ten thousand people lived at Fairview over the course of ninety-two years. Sisters, fathers, cousins, aunts vanished from their home communities. I watch a film made by a man whose younger sister disappeared. Jeff Daly was six years old, Molly Daly two, when she went missing—not even a shadow or secret to mark her departure, just a sudden unexplained absence as if she had never existed. In *Where's Molly: A True Story of Those Lost and Found*, Jeff documents his search, tracking his sister's disappearance to Fairview.[5] He follows a trail from a note found in his father's wallet to a folder tucked away in a back drawer, from a phone number in that folder to a group home in suburban Portland, from social workers at that group home to a case file complete with photos.

Along the way, he finds a promotional film made by Fairview in 1959 called *In Our Care*.[6] The grainy black-and-white footage crackles and pops. He first sees his sister here as she sits on the floor of a crowded bare room, clapping her hands and playing with a ball. Molly looks straight into the camera, eyes crooked, engaged, still inquisitive—so different from the case file photos taken later, her face defiant and shuttered. We see nurses tending children in cribs, row upon row in room after room. We see a cafeteria where a chaos of children eat, a laundry room where women fold sheets and men tend big steam dryers. We see a woman in an isolation cage. We don't see the cow whips, handcuffs, head cages, straitjackets, the threats of acid baths, the realities of rape. I contemplate what it means to describe Fairview as "not the best, but . . . certainly . . . not the worst."

In 1966 did my parents drive me to Fairview searching not only for diagnosis and cure but also a place to leave me? Did they see *In Our Care*, absorbing the narrator's cheerful authority into their body-minds, anger, relief, and shame vying for attention? When did they decide to take me home; what tipped the scale? I have no idea. I only know it was a pivotal moment that has shaped my entire life.

With some frequency, people ask: "What's wrong with you?" "What happened to you?" "What's your defect?" Or they play a guessing game: "Is it multiple sclerosis or Parkinson's, muscular dystrophy or ALS?" Usually I answer quickly, "Cerebral palsy. No, it's not progressive, and no, it's not terminal." Curiosity satiated, they move on.

I could respond with any number of diagnoses. I could deflect, "You choose. In 1966 a doctor said 'mental retardation,' and in 1976 a physical therapist said 'cerebral palsy.'" I could push, "What more do you know about me now that you have two diagnoses to attach to my body-mind?" It's much easier just to say "cerebral palsy" and move on.

Reading Diagnosis
....

It's impossible to grapple with cure without encountering white Western medical diagnosis—ink on paper in the *Diagnostic and Statistical Manual of Mental Disorders* and the *International Classification of Diseases*, a process in the hands of doctors, a system of categorization. I want to read diagnosis as a source of knowledge, sometimes trustworthy and other times suspect. As a tool and a weapon shaped by particular belief systems, useful and dangerous by turns. As a furious storm, exerting pressure in many directions.

Simply put, diagnosis wields immense power. It can provide us access to vital medical technology or shame us, reveal a path toward less pain or get us locked up. It opens doors and slams them shut.

Diagnosis names the conditions in our body-minds, charts the connections between them. It holds knowledge. It organizes visceral realities. It draws borders and boundaries, separating fluid in the lungs from high blood pressure, ulcers from kidney stones, declaring anxiety attacks distinct from heart attacks, post-traumatic stress disconnected from depression. It legitimizes some pain as real; it identifies other pain as psychosomatic or malingering. It reveals little about the power of these borders and boundaries. Through its technology—x-rays, MRIs, blood draws, EKGs, CAT scans—diagnosis transforms our three-dimensional body-minds into two-dimensional graphs and charts, images on light boards, symptoms in databases, words on paper. It holds history and creates baselines. It predicts the future and shapes all sorts of decisions. It unleashes political and cultural forces. At its best, diagnosis affirms our distress, orients us to what's happening in our body-minds, helps make meaning out of chaotic visceral experiences.

But diagnosis rarely stays at its best. It can also disorient us or devalue what we know about ourselves. It can leave us with doubts, questions, shame. It can catapult us out of our body-minds. All too often diagnosis is poorly conceived or flagrantly oppressive. It is brandished as authority, our body-minds bent to match diagnostic criteria rather than vice versa. Diagnosis can become a cover for what health care providers don't understand; become more important than our messy visceral selves; become the totality of who we are.

....

These experiences of disorientation and devaluing are often called *misdiagnosis*, as if the ambiguity and ambivalence contained within diagnosis could be resolved by determining its accuracy. But let me redirect this focus on correctness. In my reading of diagnosis, I'm not interested in whether I *really* have cerebral palsy or whether schizophrenia *accurately* characterizes the many realities of seeing visions and hearing voices. Rather I'm inviting us to think about what diagnosis does, because this system not only describes those of us deemed defective, deficient, or disordered in a million different ways but also helps shape how the world treats us.

Consider the diagnosis of mental retardation. Certainly it can name people who think, process, and communicate differently. But with that naming comes a whole host of expectations, stereotypes, and material realities. *Mental retardation* shapes where and how some people receive education. It influences the unlikelihood that they'll have paid work and homes of their own choosing. It increases the probability of having their children taken away; of landing in prison, a group home, an institution. It can also create access to services and adaptive technologies, Individualized Education Plans and job training. The diagnosis of mental retardation is often dangerous, sometimes useful, but never neutral, never merely descriptive.

....

Hundreds of forces swirl through diagnoses, each with its own balance of utility and risk. Some carry almost no stigma; others come freighted with discrimination and self-loathing; still others bring both relief and sorrow. I want to read diagnosis in all its incarnations.

Disorder

Within white Western medicine, diagnosis projects the concept and practice of *disorder* onto us. Flip through the two source books for diagnostic labels and codes (the *Diagnostic and Statistical Manual of Mental Disorders* and the *International Classification of Diseases*), and that word leaps out repeatedly to describe, define, and categorize body-minds.

Some of us do live with dis-order—digestive tracks, immune systems, neurons, nerve receptors, muscles, and joints that have fallen out of the order most typically associated with humans. Of course, this descriptive notion of dis-order relies on a clear, singular definition of order. But *disorder* means not only dis-ordered but also wrong, broken, in need of repair.

Disorder is used to constrict and confine, devalue and pathologize. Consider the hearing of voices and seeing of visions. White Western medicine defines these experiences unequivocally as symptoms of a biologically based disorder that needs to be eradicated. Within this framework, all the side effects of antipsychotic drugging—numbness, sedation, cognitive slowdown, tremoring, and twitching, along with the possibilities of heart failure, kidney failure, stroke, diabetes, and seizures—are deemed preferable to the experiences currently diagnosed as *schizophrenia*. *Disorder* doesn't allow for voices and visions to be common—connected to our daydreams or spiritual experiences, the channeling and writing of fictional characters or the terrifying aftermath of trauma. *Disorder* dictates specific ways of understanding our body-minds and excludes others.

I wonder what we would know about ourselves and each other if diagnosis projected acceptance rather than disorder onto our body-minds. Inside this imagined projection, pain and death might become familiar parts of our life cycle rather than markers of disorder to dread and avoid. Those of us who shake or hallucinate, who are fat or don't use spoken language might become ordinary rather than dangerous and undesirable. Without *disorder*, white Western medical diagnosis might not even exist.

Antibiotics and Acupuncture

The medical-industrial complex wants us to understand diagnosis as a universal truth about our body-minds, wrong only when misdiagnosis has occurred.

I've been sick for a week, coughing nonstop—huge, wracking barks. I'm so weak I can barely climb the stairs to the bathroom. The over-the-counter cold and flu medicine that I've been gulping down doesn't work. Finally, I drag myself to the doctor. All I want is to get better; I have no ambivalence about cure. The doc takes my blood pressure, temperature, and blood oxygen level; listens to my lungs and heart; unsuccessfully tries to collect a sample of what I'm coughing up. After fifteen minutes he diagnoses bronchitis, gives me prescriptions, and sends me on my way. I have health insurance and pay ten dollars for the office visit.

I love the relief that the codeine cough syrup gives me, but three doses later I'm so nauseous and dizzy I think I might pass out. It takes me twenty-four hours to recover. I start the antibiotics, and my cough lessens some. I remain weak and miserable, hacking my lungs up.

Several days pass; I drag myself to the acupuncturist. He listens to my cough; looks at my tongue; asks me about temperature, diet, and pain; checks my pulses. He says I have too much heat in my lungs and gives me a glass of warm water with herbs that taste like earth—bitter and tangy. I lie down on his table, and he places needles in my forehead, temples, upper lip, and feet. As they enter my skin, they sparkle, pierce, thump. He asks me how the needles feel. I'm at a loss for words. He nods and smiles. This middle-aged white guy who's been an herbalist for twenty-five years and an acupuncturist for ten says that in English we don't have words for what the needles do to our body-minds but that in Cantonese and Mandarin there's a myriad of words to describe this experience. I lie quietly for a long time, the needles in me. Later he gives me herbs and sends me home with another appointment. I have money beyond food and rent and pay $150 out-of-pocket.

I love the nighttime herbs. They calm my coughing and put me to sleep. My head no longer throbs; pain doesn't spike every time I cough. There are no miracles, but slowly over the next month as the antibiotics, herbs, and needles work through me, my cough diminishes and strength returns.

....

I think about these two explanations for my cough and exhaustion. On the one hand, bronchitis as a diagnosis is less than a hundred years old, emerging from the culture in which I live. The language I speak and beliefs I grew up with make it familiar. Bronchitis concerns itself with bacteria, symptoms, and acute intervention. In white Western medicine, it is understood as scientific, revealing the truth of a specific body-mind condition.

On the other hand, heat in the lungs is rooted in cultures, histories, and centuries of practice with which I have no daily connection. It deals with elements, energies, and balance. In the white Western world with its imperialist history of suppressing Indigenous systems of medicine, heat in the lungs is regarded with great skepticism.

These two diagnoses projected such different medical knowledge onto me. For a moment, I tried to make them converge, seduced by the white Western system that sells its frameworks and conclusions as the singular, definitive story about our body-minds. I wanted to figure out which one of these diagnoses was "right."

I failed but quickly realized I didn't need the *single* story that told the entire truth about my coughing and exhaustion.[7] Rather, in the midst of feeling horrible, what I wanted was increased comfort, a way to calm my lungs, and a course of treatment that led back to well-being. "Rightness" counted for almost nothing.

....

In spite of what the medical-industrial complex tells us, diagnosis is a tool rather than a fact, an action rather than a state of being, one story among many.

The Price of Diagnosis

Fairview haunts me. I listen to the histories, the decades of imprisonment, the everyday violence. Removal, isolation, restraint, beating, drugging, random torment, neglect—diagnosis set it all in motion.

In his documentary *Where's Molly*, Jeff Daly recounts how his sister Molly vanished from his life: "And one day she's gone. I'm six years old. Where'd she go? Nobody told me. . . . Molly was erased from our family." Her removal started with diagnosis.[8]

At first the doctors in her hometown said that Molly had a club foot and cataracts in one eye. She had surgery when she was nearly two. Soon after, the doctors wrote "profoundly retarded" in her case file, those two words projecting a world of stereotypes onto her body-mind. They told her parents that she'd be nothing but a vegetable, and then she disappeared to Fairview. Diagnosis justified the decisions made by her doctors, her parents, the state.

Images from the film float through me: Molly as a chubby white toddler in family photos, a five-year-old bouncing a ball and clapping her hands in Fairview's 1959 promotional film *In Our Care*, a girl in case file photos dating from 1961 to 1971, a woman thirty-five years later in a group home, sitting in a wheelchair, smiling as she celebrates her fiftieth birthday.[9] I try to conjure the years between 1957, when Molly's aunt and uncle dropped her off at Fairview, and 1991, when she moved into the group home. I don't know if I can make my imagination bleak enough. Diagnosis sustained her imprisonment.

I want to ask her: *Where did you stash your sorrow and rage? What small pleasures did you steal?* I hope she will respond, maybe not in words, but with her eyes that flash and grimace.

Needless to say, Molly's removal shaped her entire life. At the same time, her diagnosis and disappearance also marked her family. Removal is never only about the people removed. Sometimes it's a ripple, touching individuals, families, and social networks. Sometimes it's a warning, putting whole communities on edge. Sometimes it's a blunt force, uprooting entire cultures.[10]

If my parents had left me at Fairview in 1966 after the doctors declared me mentally retarded, I too would have faced decades of punishment, antipsychotic meds—probably Stelazine and Thorazine—and hard labor in the kitchen or laundry. My imagination fails.

The impact of diagnosis at Fairview didn't stop with removal. It also justified why people needed long-term care and authorized many kinds of abuse. Using head cages and straitjackets, drugging with psychotropic meds, locking people into isolation cages became means of keeping residents "safe," practices of "care" rather than forms of violence.

Grueling daily schedules were ordinary routines. In a short documentary called *Voices from Fairview*, seven white former residents talk about their time at the institution.[11] Paul Wood recounts a typical day for him in the 1960s: up at 5:30 a.m., work in the pantry before school, school during the day, an hour for lunch bracketed by work in the pantry, yet more time in the pantry after school, and finally to bed at 8:00 p.m. When asked whether he received money for his four hours of labor a day, Wood replies, "No, they [did] not pay nobody. You [got] your hair cut free and you [went] to the doctor and you [got] to live in the cottage free too. And you [got] your food free too." His unpaid work became a kind of care rather than exploited child labor, care that diagnosis made essential.

Imprisonment was taken for granted. Another former resident says, "The first time I went to Magruder [a "cottage" at Fairview], I thought, bars on the windows. I couldn't go anyplace. . . . Then I got used to it, and it was simple." Kenneth Newman calls Fairview the "gateway to hell." He remembers fighting, being locked up, and running away "more times than I can count." Shirley Newman escaped too, sometimes with Kenneth and other times with another friend. She remembers staff chasing them down, bringing them back, shackling them to their beds. Care was laced with violence, which prompted resistance, which in turn was met with more violence, all of it sustained by diagnosis.

Punishment was a regular occurrence. Shirley and Kenneth remember being tied down with leather straps, covered with wet sheets, scalded with hot water. It's impossible to regard these punishments as anything but violence. Shirley reflects, "Us girls were scared. . . . If we said something, told on somebody, we would get in trouble." Under the guise of care and shielded by diagnosis, these conditions went unchecked for many decades.

The violence set in motion by diagnosis isn't only a thing of the past. Today residents at Massachusetts's Judge Rotenberg Educational Center—a residential institution, billed as a school for youth diagnosed with a variety of body-mind conditions—endure daily electric shocks aimed at changing their behavior. As part of their "treatment" plans, many students wear ten-pound battery packs on their backs, have electrodes taped to their arms, legs, and stomachs, and are monitored twenty-four hours a day for "misbehaviors." For each transgression, staff apply two seconds of electric shock. Some residents have experienced this jolting pain dozens of times in a single day. Investigative journalist Jennifer Gonnerman likens the sensation to "a horde of wasps attacking . . . all at once."[12] Rob Santana, a former resident who spent three and a half years at Rotenberg and has also done some prison time, says, "It's worse than jail. That place is the worst place on earth."[13] Disability activists are working hard to shut the Center down, but as of 2014, electric shock was still being used on a substantial number of residents.

This violence is made thinkable and doable through diagnosis. Electric shock is framed and defended as treatment, not torture, because the residents at Rotenberg have been labeled with autism and ADHD, intellectual disability and bipolar disorder.

The price of diagnosis can be so high.

Useful, but to Whom?

It is impossible to name all the ways in which diagnosis is useful.

It propels eradication and affirms what we know about our own body-minds. It extends the reach of genocide and makes meaning of the pain that keeps us up night after night.[14] It allows for violence in the name of care and creates access to medical technology, human services, and essential care. It sets in motion social control and guides treatment that provides comfort. It takes away self-determination and saves lives. It disregards what we know about our own body-minds and leads to cure.

Diagnosis is useful, but for whom and to what ends?

STONE

Walking on one of my favorite childhood beaches—a wide, flat stretch of sand in occupied Kwatami Territory—I find a stone glistening at low tide, vivid green and black. I pick it up, rub it between my fingers, tracing its round edges, uneven surfaces. I feel its weight in my hand. Through its center, some long-ago limpet, barnacle, or steady drip of water has bored a hole—on one side a lopsided groove and on the other a small circular opening, stone slowly, slowly turning to grit. I slip it into my pocket, later thread a leather cord through the hole and wear it around my neck, green and black blurring as the stone absorbs oil from my skin.

4 NUANCES OF CURE

Wishing You Less Pain

You and I know each other through a loose national network of queer disability activists, made possible by the Internet. Online one evening, I receive a message from you containing the cyber equivalent to a long, anguished moan of physical pain. You explain that you're having a bad pain day, and it helps to acknowledge the need to howl. Before I log off, I type a good night to you, wish you a little less pain for the morning. Later you thank me for not wishing you a pain-free day. You say, "The question isn't whether I'm in pain but rather how much." As I get to know you in person, you tell me, "I read medical journals hoping for a breakthrough in pain treatment that might make a difference." You work to locate a doctor who might believe your reports of pain. Work to create the appropriate script—the exact words and stories that will open the door, lead doctors to treat you as a patient rather than a drug-seeking criminal. Work to obtain the necessary scripts—the actual prescriptions. Work to find the right balance of narcotics. You work and work and work some more.

Many a disability activist has declared that there's nothing wrong with our disabled body-minds, even as we differ from what's considered normal. I have used this line myself more than once, to which you respond, "It's true; we need to resist the assumptions that our bodies are wrong and broken. But at the same time, the chronic fatiguing hell pain I live with is not a healthy variation, not a natural bodily difference."

I grasp at the meanings of *natural* and *unnatural* again. The moments and locations where disability and chronic pain occur—can we consider them natural, as our fragile, resilient human body-minds interact with the world? Is it natural when a spine snaps after being flung from a car or a horse, when a brain processes information in fragmented ways after being exposed to lead, mercury, pesticides? Can a body-mind be deemed both natural and abnormal? I ask because I don't understand.

And when are those moments and locations of disability and chronic pain unnatural—as unnatural as war, toxic landfills, childhood abuse, and poverty?

Wanting Cure

You and I sit in a roomful of disabled people, inching our way toward enough trust to start telling bone-deep truths. You say, "If I could wake up tomorrow and not have diabetes, I'd choose that day in a heart-beat." I can almost hear your stream of thoughts: the daily insulin, the tracking of blood sugar levels, the shame, the endless doctors, the sei-zures, the long-term unknowns. You don't hate your body-mind, nor do you equate diabetes with misery. You're not waiting desperately, half-panicked. I know that all the time and money spent on research rather than universal health care, a genuine social safety net, an end to poverty and hunger pisses you off.

At the same time, you're weary of the analogies: the hope that one day AIDS will become as treatable and manageable as diabetes, the equating of transsexual hormone replacement therapy with insulin. You want to stamp your feet and demand, "Pay attention to this specific experience of type 1 diabetes—my daily dependence on a synthesized hormone, my life balanced on this chemical, the maintenance that marks every meal." You'd take a cure tomorrow, and yet you relish sitting in this room.

Birthmark

You and I talk, as we so often do, over food—this time pasta, bread, and olive oil. It would be a cliché to begin with a description of your face across from mine. Certainly I observe the vivid curve of your birthmark, its color and texture, but it doesn't become your entire being. I know from your stories that your face precedes you into the world, that one visible distinction overtaking everything else about you.

You say, "I'm wondering why at fifteen I stopped wearing thick waxy makeup. Why did I—after a childhood of medical scraping, burning, tat-tooing—still pursue laser surgery, seduced by the doctor's promises? But the excruciating pain of the first treatment made me sick, and I never went back. I don't know when I stopped cupping face in hand, shielding the color of my skin from other humans." I listen as you track your body-mind's turn away from eradication toward a complicated almost-pride. You research beauty, scrutinizing the industry of birthmark removal.

You page through medical textbooks, see faces like yours, and swallow hard against shame. You've started meeting other people with facial distinctions, talking about survival and desire, denial and matter-of-factness. Tonight you wear a bright shirt, earrings to match. You insist on your whole body-mind with all its color.

....

I don't understand: what becomes natural and normal? It genuinely mystifies me. Who decides that your purple textured skin is unnatural, my tremoring hands abnormal? How do those life-changing decisions get made?

Cautionary Tale

You and I meet at a disability community event. We end up in a long conversation about shame and love. You tell me the military dumped trichloroethylene near your childhood home, that chemical leaching into the groundwater and shaping your body-mind as you floated in utero. When you talk to people about this pollution and its impact, they mostly respond with pity, turning you and your wheelchair into a tragedy.

Your story reminds me of a series of advertisements in the Sierra Club's campaign Beyond Coal. In one, the tagline reads, "Asthma. Birth defects. Cancer. Enough," superimposed over a looming smoke-belching power plant.[1] In another, we see the big belly of a pregnant woman dressed in pink, one hand cupping her stomach. Her skin is light brown. Her face isn't visible. Her belly is captioned, "This little bundle of joy is now a reservoir of mercury." The fine print tells us: "Mercury pollution from our nation's coal-burning power plants is harming pregnant women and their unborn children. Mercury is a powerful neurotoxin that can damage the brain and nervous system—causing developmental problems and learning disabilities."[2]

To persuade viewers that these plants need to be shut down, both ads use disability to make an argument about the consequences of environmental destruction. There is so much to pull apart here about gender and race. The second ad relies on stereotypes about femininity and the supposed vulnerability of women and children. It objectifies a woman of color, reducing her to a body part, which is then further reduced to a reservoir. But at the center of this argument lies disability.

Seemingly the ads ask us to act in alliance with the people most impacted by the burning of coal.[3] But digging down a bit, the Sierra Club twists away from solidarity, focusing instead on particular kinds of body-mind conditions—asthma, birth defects, cancer, learning disabilities—transforming them into symbols for environmental damage. This strategy works because it taps into ableism. It assumes that viewers will automatically understand disability and chronic illness as tragedies in need of prevention and eradication, and in turn that these tragedies will persuade us to join the struggle.

Certainly ending environmental destruction will prevent some body-mind conditions. But by bluntly leveraging ableism, the ads conflate justice with the eradication of disability. The price disabled and chronically ill people pay for this argument is high. It reduces our experiences of breathing, of living with conditions deemed birth defects, of having cancer, of learning in many different ways to proofs of injustice. This reduction frames disability yet again as damage located entirely within individual body-minds while disregarding the damage caused by ableism. It ignores the brilliant imperfection of our lives. It declares us as unnatural as coal-burning power plants. The price of this argument would be one thing if it occurred in isolation, but the Sierra Club's rhetoric is only a single example in a long line of public health campaigns—against drunk driving, drug use, lead paint, asbestos, unsafe sex, and on and on—to use disability and chronic illness as cautionary tales.[4]

Amidst this cacophony, you want to know how to express your hatred of military pollution without feeding the assumption that your body-mind is tragic, wrong, and unnatural. No easy answers exist. You and I talk intensely; both the emotions and the ideas are dense. We arrive at a slogan for you: "I hate the military and love my body."

Undoubtedly we could have come up with a catchier or more complex slogan. Nonetheless, it lays bare an essential question: how do we witness, name, and resist the injustices that reshape and damage all kinds of body-minds—plant and animal, organic and inorganic, nonhuman and human—while not equating disability with injustice?

Body-Mind Yearning

The desire for cure, for the restoration of health, is connected to loss and yearning. What we remember about our body-minds in the past seduces us. We wish. We mourn. We make deals. We desire to return to the days before immobilizing exhaustion or impending death, to the nights thirty years ago when we spun across the dance floor. We dream about the body-minds we once had before depression descended; before we gained twenty, fifty, a hundred pounds; before our hair turned gray. We ache for the evenings curled up in bed with a book before the ability to read vanished in an instant as a bomb or landmine exploded. We long for the time before pain and multigenerational trauma grabbed our body-minds.

We reach toward the past and dream about the future, feeling grief, envy, shame. We compare our body-minds to friends and lovers, models in *Glamour* and *Men's Health*. Photoshopped versions of humans hold sway. We find ourselves lacking. The gym, diet plan, miracle cure grip us. *Normal* and *natural* won't leave us alone. We remain tethered to our body-minds of the past, wanting to transport them into the future, imagining in essence a kind of time travel.

Even without a nondisabled past tugging at me, I too find myself yearning. Occasionally I wish I could step into the powerful grace of a gymnast or rock climber, but that wish is distant, fading away almost as soon as I recognize it. Sometimes in the face of a task I can't do, frustration overwhelms me, and I long for steady, nimble hands. But in those moments, I've learned to turn away from yearning and simply ask for help. At the same time, the longing I feel most persistently centers on body-mind change. As my wrists, elbows, and shoulders have grown stiff and sore, I've had to stop kayaking. It's a small loss in the scheme of things, but I do miss gliding on the rippling surface of a lake, the rhythm of my paddle dipping in and out of the water.

Cure is such a compelling response to body-mind loss precisely because it promises us our imagined time travel. But this promise can also devalue our present-day selves. It can lead us to dismiss the lessons we've learned, knowledge gained, scars acquired. It can bind us to the past and glorify the future. It can fuel hope grounded in nothing but the shadows of *natural* and *normal*. And when this time travel doesn't work or simply isn't possible, we need a thousand ways to process the grief prompted by body-mind loss.

....

Certainly our losses are real, but so is our adaptability. People living with body-mind conditions that grow more significant over time talk about drawing lines in the sand beyond which life would be intolerable. But as their body-minds change, they find their lines also shift. Reflecting on having multiple sclerosis, essayist Nancy Mairs writes:

> Everybody, well or ill, disabled or not, imagines a boundary of suffering beyond which, she or he is certain, life will no longer be worth living. I know that I do. I also know that my line, far from being scored in stone, has inched across the sands of my life: at various times, I could not possibly do without long walks on the beach . . . ; use a cane, a brace, a wheelchair; stop teaching; give up driving; let someone else put on and take off my underwear. One at a time . . . I have taken each of these (highly figurative) steps. . . . I go on being, now more than ever, the woman I once thought I could never bear to be.[5]

What begins as loss or pure suffering frequently becomes ordinary and familiar over time. This transformation is another response to body-mind loss.

Yearning for the Peeper Pond

i.

The connections between loss, yearning, and restoration aren't only about human body-minds. Many of us mourn the vacant lots, woods, and swamps we played in as children, now transformed into landfills, strip malls, and parking lots. We fear the far-reaching impacts of climate change as hurricanes grow more frequent, glaciers melt, and deserts expand. We long for the days when bison roamed the Great Plains and Chinook salmon swam upstream in the millions. We desire a return.

And so environmentalists, partly motivated by this longing, have started to learn the art and science of ecological restoration. They broadcast tallgrass prairie seeds, raise and release wolves, bison, whooping cranes. They tear up drainage tiles and reroute water back into what used to be wetlands. They pick up trash, blow up dams, plant trees, hoping beyond hope that they can restore ecosystems to some semblance of their former selves before the white, colonialist, capitalist, industrial damage was done.

When it works, restoration can be a powerful force, contributing to the earth's well-being, as well as providing an antidote to loss. But the damage may be irreversible; some ecosystems, irreplaceable. Restoration may take centuries or may be a Band-Aid stuck onto a gaping wound. We may not be able to fix what has been broken.

ii.

Below my house on the edge of the cow pastures, there used to be a little swampy pond surrounded by cattails, where in the early spring, just after the ice melted, hundreds of peepers would breed. These small, light-brown frogs would sing through the night. Sometimes I'd walk to the pond and stand for ten or fifteen minutes, surrounded by their chorus, eardrums and chest reverberating, shoes growing soggy. Two summers ago, neighbors built a house down there. I watched the structure go up but didn't register what it might mean for the peepers. Last spring I headed down the hill as usual, tromping through the upper field, then the hedgerow, coming out at the western edge of the cow pastures. But there was no pond, no chorus of peepers abruptly stopping as I approached. I wandered around for a while, feeling disoriented, before I realized that my neighbors' backyard was exactly where the peeper pond used to be.

It's a tiny loss in the scheme of things. This patch of land, occupied Abenaki Territory, has endured so much ecological change in the almost four centuries since white people stole it. We've clearcut it three times. Fenced it with stones walls, hedgerows, barbed wire. Planted grass. Put sheep and cows out to graze. Built houses and barns in wetlands. Created manure piles. Drilled wells for water. Leaked gas. Made garbage heaps of wire, tires, railroad ties. Bulldozed roads. More than enough damage has been done, and yet many native plants and animals are somehow doing well, including the peepers. Still, I miss this particular peeper pond, yearn to stand again at its edge, listening.

There is no return to the time before my neighbors' house, before the sheep and cows, before white people arrived. Instead I carry these losses with me. I'm slowly learning the importance of bearing witness—a quiet daily recognition, so different from the desire to repair. I let these losses sit uncomfortably in my heart. At the same time, I walk in the woods. I recycle. I take to the streets to shut down the natural gas pipeline that Vermont Gas wants to build not far from here. I grow kale and beets in our backyard. I join the solar electric co-op down the road. I remember that the Abenaki Nation has not vanished, four bands making home on the land currently known as Vermont. They've relearned old traditions and are creating new ones. They've gained recognition from the state government. They've acquired, in recent years, several pieces of land, one of them an old burial site and another a sacred spot they've frequented for thousands of years. They join Indigenous peoples from all over the world in finding many ways to survive, to cultivate well-being, to defend their sovereignty.[6]

And still, there is no return to the past.

iii.

I remember my conversation with the woman whose body-mind has been shaped by military pollution, remember her slogan, "I hate the military and love my body." I sit with the question: how do we witness, name, and resist the injustices that reshape and damage all kinds of body-minds—plant and animal, organic and inorganic, nonhuman and human—while not equating disability with injustice? I feel my grief and rage over environmental losses as small as the disappearance of a single peeper pond and as big as the widespread poisoning of the planet's groundwater. I think about how we might bear witness to body-mind loss while also loving ourselves just as we are right now. I begin to understand restoration—both of ecosystems and of health—as one particular relationship between the past, present, and future.[7]

Jostling My Anti-Cure Politics

I have long brandished a vehement anti-cure politics to defend myself against the unending assertions that disability equals damage, lack of health, defect. In one diatribe, I write: "Rather than a medical cure, we want civil rights, equal access, gainful employment, the opportunity to live independently, good and respectful health care, unsegregated education. . . . Needless to say, a cure is not high on our list of goals."[8] In direct response, white queer disabled and chronically ill writer Peggy

Munson states, "This [politics] does not . . . apply to those of us who see treatment or cure as the only viable accommodations that would allow us back into society. . . . I have spent too many days in a place beyond living, watching hours of reality TV because reality has become like an interesting form of fiction to me. I am too sick to have employment, attend any school, or live independently without treatment or cure."[9] I could quibble about treatment versus cure, protest by saying that I've never been anti-treatment. But in actuality, my anti-cure politics has all too often shut out chronically ill people. I need to sit with Peggy Munson's words.

I listen again to the cancer survivor: "I'm not at war with my body, but at the same time, I won't passively let my cancerous cells have their way with me." To the woman for whom a pain-free day doesn't exist: "The chronic fatiguing hell pain I live with is not a healthy variation." To the power-chair-using friend who told me recently: "My wheelchair is a part of me that I wouldn't give up. But my lungs that threaten to kill me every time I get a cold—I would trade them in for a better pair without a second thought." I let their voices jostle my anti-cure politics.

As I listen, I feel the lived experiences of illness, disorder, debilitating pain and exhaustion—the moments when disability is in truth linked to being unhealthy—mount up. They ask me to pay attention. Disabled feminist thinker Susan Wendell writes, "Some unhealthy disabled people . . . experience physical or psychological burdens that no amount of social justice can eliminate. Therefore, some very much want to have their bodies cured, not as a substitute for curing ableism, but in addition to it."[10] She insists on all our looping realities, refusing a disability politics that denies illness. All too often, even in disability communities, chronically ill people hear: "You don't seem sick," "You can't be sick again," "It's all in your head." I let Wendell's words jostle me too.

....

Amidst these voices, I think again about the Sierra Club ads, which, while leveraging ableism, make important connections between environmental destruction and illness. They tell us unequivocally, "Pay attention: burning coal causes cancer and asthma." Frustratingly, in its current form this environmentalist message also transforms illness into a symbol. However, I can imagine a slightly different series of billboards and commercials, integrating a broad-based, multi-issue politics of chronic illness and disability. They would locate injustice in many places all at once: in coal burning; in extracting fossil fuels from the ground; in poisoning the planet and the many beings that make home here, including humans; in the racism and classism that force poor people and people of color to live and work near environmental destruction. Cancer and asthma would become not symbols but lived realities amidst injustice.

Using this broad-based, multi-issue politics as a guide, the restoration of health doesn't only involve the use of medical technology to repair a boy's lungs and return his breathing to normal or to stop the ravages of cancer in a woman's body and create permanent remission. Cure also requires dismantling racism, poverty, and environmental injustice. I let health and cure take on multiple meanings.

At the same time, in a world saturated with ableism, it's difficult to acknowledge the connections between disability, chronic illness, and injustice while also holding on to the inherent value of disabled and chronically ill people. I yearn for a future when everyone has health care that promotes well-being and self-determination; enough nourishing food to eat; access to clean, plentiful water and warm, dry, safe places to live. I long for a time after we've stopped spewing tens of thousands of human-made toxins; cleaned up the garbage dumps, radiation leaks, and oil spills; put an end to body-mind-breaking work conditions. I'm desperate for a world where war, imperialism, and genocide no longer exist, and colonial-settler nations are making ongoing reparations. In this imagined future, the body-mind differences we now call disability and chronic illness will be diminished, some of them eradicated. Yet humans are too fragile and the world too unpredictable for disabled and sick people to disappear. And if we did, what a loss that would be.

....

I let this multitude of relationships we have to disability, illness, suffering, injustice, and cure jostle me, knowing that I need this exact tangle of conflicting and overlapping conversations. Holding it all—sickness and human vulnerability, health and disability, the need for and the rejection of cure—is much harder work than writing anti-cure diatribes. And much more necessary.

Your Suicide Haunts Me

Bear, it's been over a decade since you killed yourself, and still I want to howl.[11] I feel anguish and rage rattling down at the bottom of my lungs, pressing against my rib cage. If ever my howling erupts, I will take it to schoolyards and churches, classrooms and prisons, homes where physical and sexual violence lurk as common as mealtime. I know many of us need to wail. Together we could shatter windows, bring bullies and perpetrators to their knees, stop shame in its tracks.

Once a week, maybe once a month, I learn of another suicide. They're friends of friends, writers and dancers who have bolstered me, activists I've sat in meetings with, kids from the high school down the road, co-workers and acquaintances, news stories and Facebook posts. They're queer, trans,[12] disabled, chronically ill, youth, people of color, poor, survivors of abuse and violence, homeless. They're too many to count.

Bear, will you call their names with me? It's become a queer ritual, this calling of the names—all those dead of AIDS and breast cancer, car accidents and suicide, hate violence and shame, overdoses and hearts that just stop beating. The names always begin wave upon wave, names filling conference halls, church basements, city parks. Voices call one after another, overlapping, clustering, then coming apart, a great flock of songbirds, gathering to fly south, wheeling and diving—this cloud of remembrance. Then quiet. I think we're done, only to have another voice call, then two, then twenty. We fill the air for thirty minutes, an hour, a great flock of names. Tonight, will you sit with me? Because, Bear, I can't sleep.

I remember your smile, your kindness, your compassionate and fierce politics. I remember our long email conversations about being disabled and trans. I remember a brilliant speech you gave at True Spirit, a trans gathering in Washington, DC. I remember you telling me about how you'd disappear for months at a time when your life became grim, how you'd do anything not to go to a psych hospital again. I remember your handsome Black queer trans disabled working-class self. And then, you were gone.

The details of your death haunt me. You had checked yourself in. You were on suicide watch. I imagine your desperation and suffering. I know racism, transphobia, classism colluded. The nurses and aides didn't follow their own protocols, not bothering to check on you every fifteen minutes. You were alive and sleeping at 5:00 a.m. and dead at 7:00 a.m.; at least that's what their records say. Did despair clog your throat, panic coil in your intestines? In those last moments, what lingered on your tongue? I know about your death as fleetingly as your life.

Bear, I'd do almost anything to have you alive here and now, anything to stave off your death. But what did you need then? Drugs that worked? A shrink who listened and was willing to negotiate the terms of your confinement with you? A stronger support system? An end to shame and secrecy? As suffering and injustice twisted together through your body-mind, what did you need?

I could almost embrace cure without ambivalence if it would have sustained your life. But what do I know? Maybe your demons, the roller coaster of your emotional and spiritual self, were so much part of you that cure would have made no sense. You wrote not long before your death, "In a world that separates gender, I have found the ability to balance the blending of supposed opposites. In a world that demonizes non-conformity, I have found the purest spiritual expression in celebrating my otherness."[13]

Yes, Bear. I know that truth. Your otherness was a beautiful braid—your hard-earned trans manhood looping into your Black self, wrapped in working-class smarts and resilience, woven into disability, threaded with queerness. I saw you last in an elevator at True Spirit. You told me that you were spending the weekend hanging out with trans men of color. I can still see your gleeful smile, sparkling eyes.

Friend, what would have made your life possible with all its aches and sorrows? I ask as someone who has gripped the sheer cliff face of suicide more than once. Calling the names exhausts me. Your death exhausts me. The threat, reality, fact of suicide exhausts me. Its arrival on the back of shame and isolation exhausts me. Bear, will you come sit beside me tonight? I'm too exhausted to sleep.

SHELLS

Camped on a barrier island off the Gulf Coast of Florida
in occupied Calusa Territory, I hunker over shells, riveted
by their shapes, sizes, textures. I marvel at the spirals
broken open—sunset oranges, reds, pinks. I slip a spindle
of shell into my pocket and down the beach find the same
shell alive, muscle of animal protruding, then retracting
in response to my touch. The shells taper to fragile points
thinner than my little finger. They bulge into hollow
chambers bigger than my fist, the biggest bleached white
and covered with barnacles.

I've brought a field guide with me, because I know
virtually nothing about this subtropical coastal ecosystem.
I flip through it, finding whelk, conch, cockle, in addition
to the shells I know well—sea urchin, sand dollar, scallop.
I whisper their names to myself.

I sit near a mound of shells, sift them through my
fingers, all the spirals broken except the tiniest, the hinged
shells separated at the joint between their wings. Paper
thin, milky white, ridged—mostly this mound is made of

fragments. Corkscrew of moon snail, cap of whelk, ring of urchin: I hang on to these names. But in truth, the shards are largely unnameable as the ocean grinds them back into sand. Through my fingers fall wriggling crabs. Down the beach, lanky white shore birds poke their long bills into the sand, feasting.

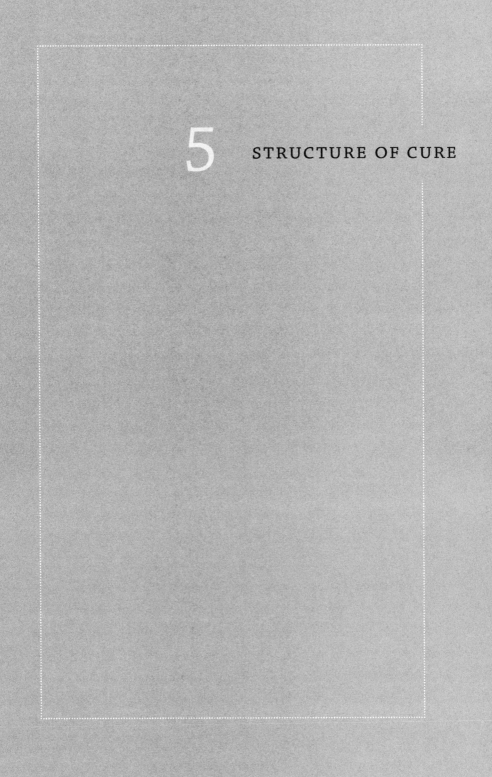

5 STRUCTURE OF CURE

The Medical-Industrial Complex

Cure as an ideology is rooted in the medical-industrial complex, which, like the military-industrial and prison-industrial complexes, is an intricate jumble.[1] Economic interests crisscross with scientific frameworks. Public and private institutions interlock. Governmental regulations sit next to cultural understandings.

The medical-industrial complex is sustained by the labor of many people, ranging from doctors to nursing home administrators, nursing aides to psychiatrists, physical therapists to researchers, scientists to marketing directors. It is located in many places all at once: community health clinics, teaching hospitals, laboratories, psychiatric facilities, medical schools, substance abuse recovery programs, Weight Watchers' meetings, pharmaceutical corporations and drug stores, Medicaid and SSI applications. Its messages are distributed by ad agencies, medical journals, and safer sex brochures. It includes nonprofit health advocacy organizations and disease- and disability-specific charity events, government agencies and public policy think tanks. Its profits are made off of health insurance and life insurance, drug sales and routine medical care, gastric bypass surgeries and kidney transplants.

The medical-industrial complex is an overwhelming thicket. It has become the reigning authority over our body-minds from before birth with prenatal testing to after death with organ donation. It shapes our understandings of health and well-being, disability and disease. It establishes sex and gender. It sets standards for normal weight and height. It diagnoses, treats, and manages the human life cycle as a series of medical events: birth, puberty, pregnancy, menopause, aging, and death, each with its own medicine.

All of our body-minds are judged in one way or another, found to be normal or abnormal, valuable or disposable, healthy or unhealthy. Our body-minds bring us pleasure and distress, sometimes needing medical care and technology to stay alive and other times needing just a little bit of improving—or so we're led to believe. In the process, most of us become reliant on the medical-industrial complex, snagged by its authority.

A Far-Reaching Network

Cure saves lives and ends lives, propels eradication and promises us that our body-minds can change. It is a tool in the drive to normalize humans, to shrink the diversity of shape, form, size, and function among us. Through cure, we believe we can control our fragile, changeable, adaptable selves. It takes the shape of medical research, medical abuse, medical healing. It plays a role in making billions of dollars of profits and in providing the most basic of health care. Amidst this cacophony, cure always revolves around the perception of a disease, infection, virus, chronic illness, dysfunction, disorder, defect, abnormality, or body-mind difference. For now, let me name this pivot "the trouble."

At its most fundamental, the ideology of cure aims to eliminate the trouble from either a single body-mind or the world at large. This eradication can be as present-day and individual as removing an infected appendix or as future-focused and collective as research targeted at ending breast cancer. The goal is to ultimately ensure that the trouble no longer exists as if it had never existed in the first place.

This ideology would be complex enough if cure functioned by itself, but it doesn't. Instead it is embedded in a network of five overlapping and interlocking medical processes—diagnosis, treatment, management, rehabilitation, and prevention. The work of cure both relies on and overshadows these other five.

Health care providers, therapists, case managers, government bureaucrats, and dozens of other kinds of workers use diagnosis to locate and name the trouble within a system of categorization developed and authorized by the medical-industrial complex. They enlist treatment to diminish the trouble, moderating its symptoms to the greatest degree possible, using medication to lower high blood pressure or make significant depression or anxiety more bearable. They piece together management strategies to make the trouble as unobtrusive as possible, finding the right balance of narcotics for chronic pain or a combination of drugs and diet to control stomach ulcers. They provide rehabilitation to restore as much body-mind function as possible after the trouble has run its course, strengthening muscles after surgery or retraining someone to speak after a stroke. And finally, they employ prevention to stop the trouble from occurring at all, keeping a community's water supply clean to stop cholera or vaccinating toddlers to stop measles or scarlet fever.

As important and necessary as diagnosis, treatment, management, rehabilitation, and prevention can be, they are not cure itself, both the benchmark and pinnacle of this network. In the end, none of the other five processes measure up. Diagnosis, however necessary to the enterprise of cure, names but doesn't change the trouble. Treatment and rehabilitation, as common stepping-stones between diagnosis and cure, approach the pinnacle. But when they're not fully successful, they leave the trouble somehow intact. Management takes the trouble's mid- or long-term existence for granted, focusing instead on symptoms. Prevention stops the trouble from entering individual body-minds or entire communities but often doesn't impact its collective existence. At the same time, none of these processes are distinct. Diagnosis and treatment blur together. Treatment and rehabilitation edge into cure. Management can be an integral part of rehabilitation. At some point, prevention extends into cure, which through it all remains the gold standard.

As a whole, this network is far-reaching. It both controls chronic pain and develops vaccines. It prescribes antidepressants and distributes safer sex guidelines. It uses chemotherapy to force cancer into remission and, in states where physician-assisted suicide is legal, makes available drugs that intentionally lead to death. It functions on an individual level and a collective level.

With its focus on eradication, cure is inflexible, in spite of being a multifaceted and contradictory cacophony. But operating in tandem with diagnosis, treatment, management, rehabilitation, and prevention, cure is quite adaptable. Together these six processes nudge, prod, and tend to our body-minds. They define and redefine *normal* and *abnormal*. They shift again and again to make a profit. They keep flexing through one another.

Troubled and Troubling Body-Minds

The trouble that the network of diagnosis, treatment, management, rehabilitation, prevention, and cure revolves around is multidimensional. Within a white Western worldview, many body-minds contain trouble.

Or they are defined entirely by trouble. Or they cause trouble. Or they are deemed both troubled and troubling.

These notions raise the question: which realities are defined as trouble by whom and for whose benefit? The answers extend far beyond exam rooms and research labs, public health policy and diagnostic codes. This query requires us to think about power and privilege, corporate greed and medical understanding. It touches on the intimate relationships we have with our own body-minds. It engages with realities played out in schools, prisons, and emergency rooms.

The answers can be straightforward and widely agreed on.

Culturally, scientifically, and materially in the dominant system of medicine in the United States, certain body-mind conditions have been easily defined as trouble—a common cold as inconvenient, bronchitis as more urgent, and pneumonia as plainly dangerous. Almost no one will disagree with these assessments. Defining body-mind trouble is seemingly simple and intuitive.

But this simplicity is a façade.

The medical-industrial complex declares muscular dystrophy to be nothing but trouble, apparently as clear-cut as pneumonia. Yet this pronouncement is simple only if we disregard voices from inside disability communities. Listen again to Harriet McBryde Johnson, born with a neuromuscular condition similar to muscular dystrophy:

> At age 15, I threw away the back brace and let my spine reshape itself into a deep twisty S-curve. Now my right side is two deep canyons. . . . Since my backbone found its own natural shape, I've been entirely comfortable in my skin. . . . I used to try to explain that . . . I enjoy my life, that it's a great sensual pleasure to zoom by power chair on these delicious muggy streets, that I have no more reason to kill myself than most people. But it gets tedious. . . . Most people don't want to know. They think they know everything there is to know just by looking at me.[2]

If she and the many other disabled people who claim comfort, pleasure, and value in our lives were heeded, it would be much more difficult, maybe impossible, to cast muscular dystrophy as unmitigated trouble to eradicate.

Too often the medical-industrial complex names our visceral experiences trouble regardless of what we know about our own body-minds. But sometimes this dynamic shifts.

I think of chronic Lyme disease, myalgic encephalomyelitis / chronic fatigue immune dysfunction syndrome (ME / CFIDS), multiple chemical sensitivities, and Gulf War syndrome. The people who live with these conditions struggle to be taken seriously. They keep saying, "Pay attention. I'm living with significant body-mind trouble. I need help." June Stein writes about this struggle, "Basically, every day I had to defend my credibility. The lack of legitimacy surrounding CFIDS came from a media who deemed my hellish reality a mere 'yuppie flu' and a government that flat-out denied its existence.... Over and over again, for nine years, I have been trying to convince others that though my cheeks are pink and rosy, ... I am horribly sick."[3]

Inside this climate of disbelief, people with conditions deemed not real are told by Veterans Affairs, their family doctors, specialists, emergency rooms that all their symptoms are imaginary. Lesbian activist and writer Joan Nestle, who in her forties became sick with ME/CFIDS, reports: "As the years passed, I learned to live with this chronic state of 'feeling poisoned,' as one woman so powerfully put it at a Long Island support group. I saw doctors as problems came up, like high blood pressure or headaches, skin rashes or stomach pains, telling them when they took [my medical] history that I had chronic fatigue syndrome or whatever name it was being called that year. Some just laughed and said there was no such thing; others said *we have no idea what that means.*"[4] Doctors offer people with chronic Lyme and multiple chemical sensitivities antidepressants. Media run reports about people pretending to be sick or disabled. Cultural critics write books naming ME/CFIDS and Gulf War syndrome hysteria.[5]

On the one hand, people with muscular dystrophy resist the notion of body-mind trouble as it is repeatedly foisted on them, and on the other hand, people with ME/CFIDS work overtime to have their body-mind trouble acknowledged while doctors and the media ignore and trivialize it. These two dynamics appear to be opposites, but actually they converge, pivoting on the ways the medical-industrial complex wields authority and dismisses what we know about our own visceral experiences.

Indeed, who defines which realities as body-mind trouble? Sometimes the answers are multiple and conflicting.

I think of the contentious issue of height, especially boyhood shortness. Is being too short body-mind trouble, particularly in the absence of health issues (however they might be defined) and material conditions such as malnutrition? The answers are conflicting. Eli Lilly, makers of synthetic human growth hormone (HGH), has one answer. Some doctors and parents agree with the pharmaceutical company; others don't. Short statured people, both children and adults, have a mix of answers. The organization Little People of America has yet another response.

At best, the determinations of body-mind trouble are fraught.

So much hangs on these definitions, including millions of dollars of profit. Over the last sixty years, the pharmaceutical corporations that sell HGH have framed shortness as grave trouble that must be addressed as early as possible in a child's—particularly a boy's—life. They've actively worked to expand the market for their drugs, shifting the criteria used to determine who is unacceptably short. In 2003 Eli Lilly petitioned the U.S. Food and Drug Administration (FDA) and won approval to sell HGH for use not only by children who are short because of a diagnosable "disorder" but also by those in the bottom 1.2 percent of height for their age group. This change added 400,000 potential customers to Eli Lilly's market. Three years after this decision, the HGH drug Humatrope made $460 million, up 40 percent from 2002.[6] All of this means that redefining the body-mind trouble of shortness increased Eli Lilly's earnings by $130 million.

Sometimes the response to the question, which realities are defined as trouble by whom and for whose benefit? is transparent. And other times, the answers are considered so intuitively obvious that no one bothers to articulate them.

I think of heterosexuality, whiteness, and wealth, particularly when two or more of these conditions exist together. The high rates of neglect and violence in heterosexual nuclear families could easily be defined as trouble. The multigenerational delusion that white people hold about our superiority could definitely qualify as trouble. The hoarding of resources in upper-middle-class and upper-class homes, as reflected by an overabundance of clothing, cars, houses, food, money, and lavish vacations, could undoubtedly meet the criteria for trouble. And yet the "heterosexual nuclear family disorder," the "white entitlement syndrome," and the "wealthy greed dysfunction" haven't been invented.[7] Nor do I actually want them to be. *Disorder*, *syndrome*, and *dysfunction* have been used against far too many people.

Still heterosexuality, whiteness, and wealth simply aren't defined as trouble. I feel almost silly writing something so obvious. And yet in a world where queer and trans people, people of color, and poor people pay an intense price every day for being deemed troubled and troubling, this obvious state of affairs needs to be called out. Queer and trans youth are kicked out of their families and homes. Immigrants of color are detained and deported in record numbers. Black men are four times more likely than white people to be diagnosed with schizophrenia. Poor people are called lazy, shiftless, and demonized for their poverty. The consequences for being deemed troubled and troubling pile up fast. And through it all, heterosexuality, whiteness, and wealth escape undiagnosed, no one locked up or kicked out solely because they're straight or white or rich.

Many answers to the question of who defines which realities as body-mind trouble are bound up with power and privilege.

....

The relationship between cure and trouble is entirely enmeshed. In *Normal at Any Cost*, the journalists Susan Cohen and Christine Cosgrove tell the story of HGH, Eli Lilly, and how girlhood tallness and boyhood shortness became known as trouble. Midway through the book, they write, only partly tongue in cheek, "Sometimes cures went in search of diseases."[8]

If muscular dystrophy wasn't deemed trouble, the last fifty years of research sponsored and encouraged by the Muscular Dystrophy Association wouldn't exist. If being gay, lesbian, or bi wasn't defined as trouble, ex-gay conversion therapy wouldn't exist. If being a person of color wasn't considered trouble, skin lighteners wouldn't exist. And if synthetic HGH didn't exist, "non-growth-hormone-deficient short stature" (the phrase Eli Lilly used at the FDA hearing) wouldn't be framed as trouble.[9]

Cure both depends on and creates body-mind trouble in all of its different forms.

Variations on Cure

Once the medical-industrial complex has defined, named, or created trouble, we as clients, patients, and consumers don't face a singular monolithic intervention. As an ideology, cure presents an inflexible set of values. But as a multifaceted and contradictory practice, it multiplies into thousands of different technologies and processes. Each variation comes with its own cluster of risks and possibilities.

Some medical technology works most of the time for most people. The use of antibiotics for infection, synthetic insulin for diabetes, synthetic estrogen and testosterone for trans folks who need or want to reshape our gendered and sexed body-minds all produce reliable and consistent results.

Other kinds of technology offer glimmers of possibility but present high risks or ambiguous outcomes. Will chemotherapy and radiation eradicate the cancer, push it into remission, buy a bit more time, or just create more misery? Will operating on the brain tumor stop the seizures and end the brain-exploding pain, or will it decrease the pain a bit and probably cause vision impairment?

Still other cures and treatments are boondoggles or experiments. When the growth hormone treatment, the hip-stabilizing operation, the $1,000-per-month regimen of vitamins and herbs goes awry, leaving us chronically ill, even more mobility impaired, or in debt, we sometimes reflect back and pinpoint how we were taken for a ride. Or we feel gratitude for the risk that changed our body-minds for the better.

And then there are the imaginary cures. I think of my parents' unending desire to repair me. It was nothing but a fantasy fueled by shame and grief. Although the medical-industrial complex has been known to manipulate people's hopes and desires, no one, except the evangelical Christians who prayed over me, ever offered my parents the possibility of an actual cure for mental retardation or cerebral palsy. Pure imagination drove my mother and father.

....

The medical-industrial complex is unwavering in its commitment to cure's ultimate goal—ensuring that body-mind trouble no longer exists as if it had never existed in the first place. Yet in practice there is a routine acceptance of potential cures, partial cures, and failed cures. I think of fat people and all the technology designed to make them slender: fad diets, prescription weight loss drugs, gastric bypass and lap band surgeries. In a fatphobic culture, it doesn't seem to matter that dieting, more often than not, results in weight cycling rather than long-term weight loss. Nor does it matter that surgery outcomes range widely—from death to permanent difficulty with eating, nutrition, and digestion; from significant long-term weight loss to weight loss followed by weight gain. The quest for slenderness, for an eradication of fatness, is seemingly worth all the failures, dangers, dubious medical procedures, and direct harm.[10]

The unquestioned value placed on cure in general provides cover for all the variations, whether they be reliable, risky, ambiguous, experimental, boondoggles, or imaginary. And when cure plainly fails, we—the consumers, clients, or patients—are often blamed, either subtly or blatantly, for these failures. We didn't try hard enough. We were lazy. We were drug resistant. We were noncompliant. Or we're told that if only we wait, a reliable cure will emerge sometime in the future. Somehow, amidst it all, the very notion of cure remains undisputed.

Skin Lighteners and Hot Springs

The tools of cure include cochlear implants and skin bleaching creams, vaccinations and hot springs. Many of these technologies are embedded in the medical-industrial complex—produced by pharmaceutical corporations; matched with users through diagnosis and treatment; shaped by researchers, doctors, and health insurance companies; and distributed by pharmacists. However, cure also extends beyond what is considered medical, some of its tools existing in cosmetic drawers and spas.

Skin bleaching products are designed to answer the trouble of dark skin. Sociologist Amina Mire lays it out clearly: "Throughout western colonial history . . . the dark body has been represented [by the dominant culture] as the least virtuous and aesthetically least appealing. . . . Constructing colonized people's culture and body images as pathological, backward and . . . ugly has been central to . . . white supremacy."[11] In other words, the trouble of skin color is created fundamentally through racism and bolstered by the medical-industrial complex's notion of pathological.

In cure's long tradition, this declaration of trouble paves the way for selling repair. Feminist scholar Margaret Hunter writes, "Women and men of color have ever-increasing opportunities to alter their bodies toward whiteness. They can purchase lighter-colored contact lenses for their eyes; they can straighten kinky or curly hair; they can have cosmetic surgeries on their lips, noses, or eyes. But one of the oldest traditions of this sort is skin bleaching."[12] Products used for this purpose are called Ambi Fade Cream, Esotérica, Porcelana, Vantex, Venus de Milo. They are claimed to lighten, brighten, and whiten the skin. They are marketed to dark-skinned women of color with taglines like "Fair and Lovely" and increasingly to dark-skinned men of color with promises like "Fair and Handsome." Sold exclusively as beauty aids, some of these creams are nonetheless available only by prescription, existing on the boundary between cosmetics and pharmaceuticals. Many of them are made with toxic, body-mind-damaging chemicals strictly regulated or banned by the FDA. But ultimately they are only loosely connected to the medical-industrial complex, in need of neither diagnostic categories nor medical authorization to sustain themselves.

The market for these creams is rooted in racist-sexist definitions of beauty and depends on women (and men) of color who have internalized the notion that the darkness of their skin is wrong and troubling. One twenty-two-year-old, when asked why she's willing to risk her health to lighten her skin, responds, "I want people to think I am more than a ghetto girl. . . . I want to walk into dance halls and feel like a movie star, a white one."[13] To be blunt, the manufacturers of skin lighteners profit from shame.

The products and treatments sold to us to fix what is deemed broken, wrong, or shameful range widely. Some, like skin lighteners, are designed for this purpose. Others, like hot springs and fresh air, are adopted.

I think of the water in Warm Springs, Georgia, and Saratoga Springs, New York; the air in Brattleboro, Vermont, and Saranac Lake, New York. Disabled and sick people with enough money to travel have long taken to the road, looking for cure, comfort, or both. They've landed at the Georgia Warm Springs Foundation, the Brattleboro Hydropathic Establishment, the Adirondack Cottage Sanitarium, the Roosevelt Bathhouses. Water bubbles hot from the ground, oozes up laden with calcium bicarbonate, sodium chloride, carbon dioxide. Air wafts fresh and cool. Travelers have arrived to soak, breathe, and restore.

At Warm Springs, they occupied hospital beds for months at a time, coped with multiple surgeries, cried themselves to sleep at night, wrestled with pain, misery, loneliness. They completed their physical therapy routines in pools heated by the springs. Some polio survivors relearned to walk; many did not. At Saranac Lake, they rested eight hours a day outside on porches, breathing the air that supposedly cured tuberculosis. Some of them lived; others died. At Brattleboro, they lay wrapped in water-soaked sheets, shivering and sweating, drank gallons of water, floated in private baths, lived half their time outdoors, taking in the good air. Some left revived, feeling better for their sojourn; others did not.

The Kanien'kehá:ka (Mohawk), Creek, Cherokee, and Abenaki used to frequent these places, lie in their waters, each nation with its own healing rituals and spiritual traditions. On this land, white people have built resorts frequented by other white people; employed African Americans as cooks, maids, chauffeurs; sold physical therapy, water therapy, fresh-air therapy. At the same time, many Indigenous peoples have been removed from these homelands. They've died of tuberculosis and smallpox; become disabled by war, hunger, poverty, alcohol, heartsickness. They've continued on, practicing and adapting their traditional systems of medicine.

....

I take a trip to Saratoga Springs, wanting to indulge in a long warm soak. Hot water relaxes my body-mind in a way that nothing else does, tremor and tension dissolving into the heat. I join the many people who, over the centuries, have flocked to these mineral baths. I expect the New Age aroma therapy and the outlandish hourly rates but not the big, old brick buildings that look like state-run hospitals and psych facilities.

I stop at a bathhouse built in 1935, named after the first, and to-date only, wheelchair-using U.S. president, who had an abiding interest in the power of water to cure. After his bout with polio, Franklin D. Roosevelt took to the road both hopeful and desperate, following rumors of healing waters at a resort in Warm Springs, Georgia. It only took him a few days in the eighty-eight-degree pools to declare progress after years of searching. A wealthy, white northerner, he bought the seventeen-hundred-acre resort in 1927, transforming it into a rehabilitation center and gathering spot for white polio survivors. The old photos show rooms full of disabled people and their mobility equipment—high-backed wheelchairs, canes and crutches, rolling beds, braces. Everyone is white, except the people cooking and cleaning. Black polio survivors went to Tuskegee, Alabama. Although he never found a cure, Roosevelt surely benefited from that disability accessible community and the warm, buoyant waters running under Pine Mountain. Years later as president, he helped find the money to fund the building of bathhouses near the curative waters of Saratoga Springs in his home state.

Stepping into the still-open-and-operating Roosevelt Bathhouse, my gait lopsided and rattling, I wonder if the staff thinks I'm yet another traveler, desperate to "take the cure." I'm looking for comfort and the delicious feeling of warm mineral water on my skin, but they may expect I want to be fixed. I've left my crip pride button at home.[14] A wooden wheelchair, wool blanket draped over one arm, decorates the lobby, even though there are two steps to get in and no sign of a ramp. Nor do I see any acknowledgment that we are on Kanien'kehá:ka land. The woman at the front desk tells me she has no more openings for the day. It's just as well. I don't really want to spend money at this place that turns a profit by selling mineral water from deep inside the planet, capitalizing on our need for comfort and desire for cure.

....

Encounters with the ideology of cure can be as daily as a cosmetic cream and as comforting as a long soak in hot mineral water, as life-saving as antibiotics and as difficult as chemotherapy, as nonmedical as the fresh air in Brattleboro and Saranac Lake and as medicalized as liver transplant surgery. No one technology epitomizes this ideology. Rather it latches on to many different tools, some of them as old as the planet and others on the cutting edge of science.

HERMIT CRABS

I hunker down among the rocks at low tide to watch a pool dotted with snails. Their shells are gray, russet, midnight blue, tightly curled. There are no signs of life among the lacy fronds of seaweed. But as I watch, the shells begin to move, not the slow, smooth motion of snails but a rapid scuttling. What! Then I recognize hermit crabs, a dozen of them. They don't grow their own shells but adopt the empty ones of other sea creatures. I sit still for the longest time watching these crabs prance and scurry, but the moment I move, they freeze, the pool yet again dotted with unmoving snail shells.

6 HOW CURE WORKS

Cure Just around the Corner

i.

I have a long history with orthopedists, the doctor of choice for kids with cerebral palsy. Every time my parents went searching for a cure, I landed in an orthopedic office, where a doc would test my reflexes, flex my joints, watch me walk. They occasionally suggested an array of surgeries and often sent me to physical therapy. I've been to state-run institutions and research facilities, teaching hospitals and rehab units. Regardless of location, the routine has stayed the same.

The last time I saw an orthopedist was over a decade ago. My neck and shoulders had been chronically sore for several years. I'd wake up some mornings unable to turn my head, hot spasms rippling under my left shoulder blade, the vertebrae in my neck too tender to touch. I usually popped ibuprofen by the handful and moved through my day gingerly, always searching for the one miraculous position that would give me some moments of relief. On really bad mornings, I called in sick to work, stayed in bed, pulled out the heating pad, and doped myself up on muscle relaxants. Finally I went to an orthopedist, wanting to hurt less and wondering about arthritis. He ran all the usual tests. I squeezed his fingers, pushed against his hands, walked across the room and back. He tapped my knees and elbows, watched my gait, manipulated my head, poked at my shoulders. He was nice enough, making eye contact and talking directly to me. He reassured me that all my pain was muscular, not skeletal, wrote me an unsurprising prescription for physical therapy, and sent me on my way.

As I headed out of his office, he added, "You know, in ten years we'll be able to use micro–brain surgery to minimize, or even end, your tremors." I stopped, retorting to myself, "Not over my dead body. You can't even explain what happens between my brain and my muscles." The next day I recounted the visit to a friend, saying with a laugh, "Yeah, right, in a decade." It took me weeks to recognize the gap between my desire for less pain and the doctor's desire for cure.

I ended up in physical therapy for six weeks, adoring the wet heat, tolerating the ice, and refusing traction. Maybe it helped. More than a decade later I've not heard about any breakthroughs in micro–brain surgery for folks with cerebral palsy, nor am I waiting.

ii.

For many decades, we've been promised cures just around the corner. Consider the Muscular Dystrophy Association (MDA). The organization churns out fund-raising ads enthusing about how close scientists are to finding a cure for muscular dystrophy. In one, a pretty white girl is photographed in black and white, her hands curled under her chin, big dark eyes staring into the distance, her wheelchair visible but downplayed. The tagline reads, "In dreams she runs . . . Muscular dystrophy must be stopped—and it will be."[1] In a another, more recent ad, they've switched to color photography, dropped the child model, and revised the familiar "Don't Walk" signal to read, "Can't Walk," The tagline declares, "With enough hope and help, this light will change."[2] The MDA just keeps on asking for money for cure.

The premise that muscular dystrophy must be eradicated is always presented as an inarguable truth. But this seeming imperative is actually an arbitrary cultural value that arises from prioritizing walking over rolling, devaluing disability and disabled people, and fearing the possibilities of death that come with some, but not all, forms of muscular dystrophy. Even if we accept the notion that the world will be a better place without this body-mind condition, the girl in the black-and-white MDA ad still has a life to live here and now, a life that will be made better by material and attitudinal access.

....

The quest to eliminate muscular dystrophy is a commitment to the future, projecting values and priorities into the months, years, and decades to come. This agenda is reflected in cure research more generally, whether it's focused on preventing polio or ending the AIDS epidemic.

Certainly these endeavors have saved many lives. AIDS, syphilis, and tuberculosis no longer predictably kill people, at least those who have access to the treatments or cures. At the same time, we mustn't ignore the ways in which research's future-focused commitment has served to devalue people in the present—for instance, treating wheelchair users with muscular dystrophy as tragic and vilifying HIV-positive pregnant women, who might pass the virus on to their children.

If the U.S. government and nonprofit organizations, private corporations and university laboratories are going to dedicate money and time to the future, they also need to do so for the present. They need to fund accessible buses, schools, classrooms, movie theaters, restrooms, housing, and workplaces. They should support campaigns to end bullying, employment discrimination, social isolation, and the ongoing institutionalizing of disabled people with the same enthusiasm with which they implement cure research. I want money for accessible playgrounds, tree houses, and sandboxes so that wheelchair-using kids aren't left twiddling their thumbs in the present while they dream of running in the future.

If we choose to wait for the always-just-around-the-corner cures, lavishing them with resources, energy, and media attention, we risk suspending our present-day lives. The belief in cure tethers us not only to what we remember of our embodied selves in the past but also to what we hope for them in the future. And when those hopes are predicated on cure technology not yet invented, our body-minds easily become fantasies and projections.

....

What do we need to make peace with our visceral selves today, to let go of the fantasies, even if we hope beyond hope that our flesh and bones, organs and neurons might be different someday down the line? I ask because I don't know the answers.

iii.

When nondisabled folks ask me whether I'd take the imaginary cure pill for cerebral palsy, they're inviting me to engage in fantasy on so many levels. That technology doesn't exist, nor is it in the making, unlike the promised cures for breast cancer, diabetes, autism. The question is nothing but a thought experiment that underlines the devaluing of disability.

I know what my answer is supposed to be. My questioners expect me to say, "Yes, of course, I'd take that pill in a heartbeat." And when I don't, they're puzzled and disbelieving. They wonder if I protest too much or am defending myself against the unpleasant truth of my misery. How can I possibly not want a cure?

It's simple. Having shaky hands and shaky balance isn't as awful as they imagine, even when I slip, totter, descend stairs one slow step at a time. My relationship to gravity is ambivalent. On mountain trails, I yearn to fly downhill, feet touching ground, pushing off, smooth and fluid. Instead on steep stretches I drop down onto my butt and slide along using both my hands and feet, for a moment becoming a four-legged animal. Only then do I see the swirl marks that glaciers left in the granite, tiny orange newts climbing among the tree roots, otherworldly fungi growing on rotten logs. My shaky balance gives me this intimacy with mountains.

I would lose so much if that imaginary cure pill actually existed. Its absence lets me be unequivocal. It opens the door to brilliant imperfection.

Charity Events

People volunteer in droves to fund-raise for their favorite charity organizations by biking, running, swimming, or walking. Many of these nonprofits are disease- and disability-specific groups lodged within the medical-industrial complex. They raise money for dozens of conditions—AIDS, breast cancer, diabetes, Crohn's disease, multiple sclerosis, lupus, and autism, to name a few. Most of the funds are funneled toward research, cure, and the future.[3]

We're not running to fund research into the connections between environmental degradation and cancer, military pollution and genetic differences; we're not cycling to ensure everyone has health insurance. The organizational agendas of these charities mostly prioritize research for treatment and cure over broad-based access to medical care, housing, education, and employment. They focus on the future rather than the present. They promote eradicating diseases and disorders from both individual body-minds and the world at large. They rarely mention the need for social justice.

Folks who volunteer to raise money for cure are asked to push themselves hard, often extending to the edges of their physical limits. They run 26.2 miles, cycle a hundred, dance all night in the name of hope or "conquering" a disease. Actually this kind of fund-raising depends on potential donors being impressed or inspired by the fund-raiser's commitment to some athletic and daunting feat. To participate, one needs to be fit, focused, and for the most part able-bodied. There aren't an overwhelming number of events capitalizing on nonathletic recreation to raise money. These charity organizations don't hold knit-a-thons, poetry bashes, and cooking competitions. Their fund-raising strategy arises from a culture drenched in extreme sports and adrenaline-producing entertainment, a culture more likely to contribute money to running than knitting, cycling than poetry, a culture obsessed with individual heroism and inspiring acts.

Much of this money-raising is motivated by fear. In one video, promoted by the nonprofit Autism Speaks, autism is personified as a villain. With ominous music in the background, he threatens parents of autistic children: "I will plot to rob you of your children and your dreams. I will make sure that every day you wake up, you will cry, wondering, 'Who will take care of my child after I die?' And the truth is, I am still winning, and you are scared. And you should be."[4] Without apology or nuance, Autism Speaks peddles the idea that autism is a terrifying, life-draining disorder.

In another video, more explicitly connected to fund-raising, we watch a child slide underwater, drowning, as the narrator intones, "Cystic fibrosis fills your lungs with fluid, makes every breath a struggle. It's like drowning on the inside. Help us stop CF swallowing young lives. Be a lifeline. Be the reason someone with cystic fibrosis keeps breathing."[5] The Canadian Cystic Fibrosis Foundation plays the same game as Autism Speaks and then directly uses the alarm it cultivates in its fund-raising pitch.

Fear makes volunteering to run 26.2 miles or bike a hundred even more compelling. Folks are not only making the future better and helping "conquer" a disease or disability. They are also taking action against individual and collective fear.

....

At the same time, it's worth paying attention to the few charity events that don't play to fear and that fold social justice into their missions. Every August since 2009, runners and walkers, wheelchair users and entire families have gathered along Lake Champlain in Burlington, Vermont, for Zoe's Race. People roll, walk, and run either one kilometer through Oakledge Park or five kilometers along the waterfront, fund-raising to make homes more disability accessible.

Erika Nestor founded the event after she and her family renovated their home to make it more accessible for her disabled daughter, Zoe.

Along the way, she learned just how expensive this kind of remodeling is and how little funding exists to help people make it happen. So she went to work, envisioning a fund-raising event to make accessibility renovations possible for families who can't afford them and organizing what has become an annual run. She partnered with a local agency that provides services to disabled people and enlisted a volunteer architect to design the modifications families need, ranging from ramps to roll-in showers. Over the years, she, along with a whole team of people, has orchestrated everything from sponsorships to food, race logistics to publicity. Between 2009 and 2014, the nearly $120,000 raised by Zoe's Race has funded the remodel of fifteen homes.[6]

Differences abound between this fund-raising effort and most other disability charity events. Zoe's Race is motivated by the value of accessibility rather than cure. The money raised goes to something concrete, improving people's present-day lives, rather than something intangible centered on the future. It offers practical help to families in the local community rather than supporting a national effort that impacts research. The website for Zoe's Race doesn't mention a single specific diagnosis. This absence is only notable because of how cure-based charities brandish diagnosis, creating organizational identities out of specific disabilities and body-mind conditions. Erika Nestor and the other event organizers know that access needs aren't defined by diagnostic categories. They don't ask people to push their limits to participate. Instead they emphasize fun, food, and music.

....

For now, the cure-based charity events hold sway. It's much easier to find a pink-ribbon run to end breast cancer than a Zoe's Race. The significant differences between the two kinds of events underline how intensely charities set up cure as the one and only response to the realities of body-mind difference and loss, placing value in the future. But Zoe's Race reminds us that the values underpinning the disability- and disease-based events aren't inevitable. We can shift our focus from cure to access, or hold the two in tandem, insisting that our present-day body-minds are as important as any vision of the future.

Shifting Technologies

There are days when my shoulders and neck are tense beyond tense, muscles spasming, days when I want to complete a mundane task but my hands won't cooperate, days when people's gawking and prurient curiosity are just too much. On those days, I might consider taking the imaginary cure pill. If it wasn't hypothetical and didn't come with too many side effects, it could be quite tempting.

In exploring our varied relationships to cure, we need to take into account what is hypothetical and what exists right now. We must span the differences between the well-established polio vaccine and the still emerging HIV drugs, between the much-touted, future-focused muscular dystrophy research and the fantasy cure pill for cerebral palsy. Many medical technologies shift over time, moving from imaginary to real, ambiguous to reliable. Through these transformations, the ways we choose—or are forced—to engage with the ideology of cure often evolve.

I think about the fraught and shifting relationships Deaf communities have with cochlear implants (CIs).[7] Many Deaf people claim themselves not as disabled but as a linguistic minority. They locate the trouble they experience not in their inability to hear but in the non-deaf world's unwillingness to learn and use sign language. They live in strong, vibrant Deaf communities. They remember the decades when American Sign Language (ASL) was actively suppressed and children were punished at school for signing. From this Deaf viewpoint, CIs aren't a welcome technological development, in part because they bring with them the non-deaf world's hope of eradicating both deafness as a medical condition and being Deaf as an identity.

Cochlear implants don't meet the benchmark of cure. They neither eradicate hearing loss from the world at large nor restore individual deaf people to "normal" hearing, casting out all the telltale signs of the former trouble. Nonetheless, they are sold as an effective and necessary treatment that approaches cure. Their marketing often targets non-deaf parents of young deaf children. These sales pitches rely heavily on the notion that not hearing is an "unbearable loss" located within individual "abnormal" ears.

The manufacturer Cochlear writes on its website about the urgency of correcting hearing loss: "There isn't a moment to waste. The younger your child receives a cochlear implant, the easier it will be for him or her to learn to hear and speak." They create pressure by emphasizing the notion of normal. They continue, "The first two years of your child's life are especially important in the development of their crucial language, speech and communication skills. Research shows that children who are fit with appropriate amplification before six months old can develop language skills on a par with their hearing peers. Older children with hearing loss miss out on this chance to catch up with children who have *normal* hearing" (emphasis added).[8] By "language, speech and communication skills," Cochlear assuredly does not mean signing or bilingual proficiency in both spoken English and ASL. Hearing and speaking orally hold the primary value. This sales pitch unabashedly uses the ideology of cure, essentially telling parents that "we will make your child normal."

When implants became available in the mid-1980s, Deaf communities argued that CIs were simply another way of stealing people, particularly children, away from thriving Deaf cultures. Researcher Julie Mitchiner writes, "I used to oppose strongly the idea of deaf people getting cochlear implants. It indicates the need to 'fix' the problem. I felt betrayed and angry that doctors implanted deaf children. What does this say about me? It tells me that there is something wrong with me. Being deaf is natural to me, and putting 'machines' inside children's heads frightened me. I believed that it would destroy deaf children's sense of pride."[9] Stories of implants causing facial paralysis, dizziness, and debilitating headaches traveled through the deaf world. Raylene Paludneviciene and Raychelle L. Harris report, "The death of some deaf children after cochlear implantation due to meningitis and the lack of appropriate preventative vaccination . . . gave rise to fears that CIs could cause more deaths. Many felt access to spoken language was not worth the perceived risk."[10] Simply put, many deaf people were refusing the ideology of cure, framing their arguments as if they could stop this onslaught of new technology.

....

Actual cure exerts different pressures and demands different responses than hypothetical cure. Let me imagine for a moment that the pill to cure cerebral palsy has been developed, manufactured, and marketed and is now widely prescribed. In this world, I see ads for the drug on a daily basis. Every time I go to my family doctor, she provides me unsolicited information about the medication and offers to write a prescription. At work, my boss passes me articles about it occasionally. The original pill was quite harsh, but five generations of research and development later, there are many fewer significant side effects. Friends with cerebral palsy similar to mine have started taking the drug and like the results. I have health insurance that covers most of the costs, making it nearly affordable. In this imagined world, the pill would come with pressures, temptations, and unknowns, to which I have no idea how I'd respond.

....

Over the last thirty years as CIs have become more effective and widespread, deaf responses have grown more varied. There are people who maintain staunch resistance and have developed the idea of Deaf-gain, pushing back against the long-standing non-deaf notion of hearing *loss*. This framework celebrates the importance of being deaf. It lays out how Deaf ways of being, thinking, and communicating make necessary contributions to both the non-deaf world and human diversity as a whole.[11]

There are people who have significant reservations about CIs for young deaf children but have accepted the increasing number of adults who choose implantation for themselves and report a wide range of outcomes. There are people who have arrived at an understanding of implants as assistive technology. Julie Mitchiner reflects on her own changing attitudes: "The biggest misconception was that cochlear implants would change deaf children, and they would not maintain a sense of deaf pride. [But] I began to realize that cochlear implants are simply tools."[12]

There are a growing number of non-deaf and deaf parents choosing CIs for their deaf and hard-of-hearing children. There are teachers—both Deaf and non-deaf allies—who are continuing their work of fostering bilingual teaching methods and classrooms, focused now in part on ensuring that implanted deaf children learn both ASL and spoken English. One deaf mother whose child has a CI sums up many of these shifts. She says, "We can't stop CIs from happening. People think we can stop it completely. It is not possible. It won't happen. Let's put it aside. We should shift our focus more to how we keep ASL alive. I think the key is to make everyone understand that the child with a CI is still deaf. These children still will miss out in a spoken language environment. ASL still provides full access to a language."[13]

These varied, and sometimes contradictory, responses to CIs are all strategies of resistance. The dominant cultural belief that being deaf is abnormal and inferior, coupled with evolving technology that brings the possibility of cure closer to the present, exerts so much pressure. Deaf and hard-of-hearing people think, sign, and write about Deaf-gain. They ambivalently accept implantation among deaf adults. They develop an understanding of CIs as one tool among many to create language access. They continue to foster bilingual education. And all the while, the non-deaf world remains invested in hearing loss as a medical disorder and implants as a near cure, the medical-industrial complex forging ahead.

....

Cure technology keeps evolving, but the ideology behind it stays the same, valuing some body-minds and devaluing others. This dynamic often intensifies the forces placed on people deemed troubled. It makes questions about the worth of disabled and deaf people more urgent. It impacts the ways in which entire communities defend themselves.

And yet many of us also need and yearn for shifts in cure technologies. In the two years before my friend H. died of ovarian cancer, repeated rounds of chemotherapy made her extraordinarily sick. We would have done nearly anything for cancer treatment to take a sudden leap forward. When my partner's sister N. was diagnosed with late-stage colon cancer, she desperately wanted to be part of a clinical trial of some experimental treatment. She knew that existing technology wasn't enough to keep her alive, much less cure her. She was right. My friend B. died of AIDS in 1993, two years before the first generation of antiretroviral drugs became available, drugs that reliably extend the lives of people with HIV. If those meds had been developed sooner and if B. had been able to afford them, he might still be alive.

....

All these realities, ranging from the ways the CIs exert pressure on deaf people to the longing for more-effective cancer treatments, exist at the same time. Like cure itself, the evolution of its technologies sparks ambivalence. We fear the shifts. We resist them. We welcome them. We need them.

A Pharmaceutical History of Eflornithine

Cure serves many purposes: saving lives, manipulating lives, prioritizing some lives over others, making profit. Consider for instance the pharmaceutical history of eflornithine.

This drug successfully cures the late stages of African trypanosomiasis, commonly known as sleeping sickness—a central African, flyborne disease characterized by pain, neurological symptoms, and sleep disturbances. If left untreated, the illness always leads to death; it kills thousands of people per year. In 1990 the drug company Marion Merrell Dow received approval from the U.S. Food and Drug Administration for eflornithine under the trade name Ornidyl. At that point, the only alternative was a harsh arsenic-based drug that sometimes itself caused death. In contrast, eflornithine revived people in the last stage of sleeping sickness, some of them already in a coma. It became known as the "resurrection drug," a nickname that reflected the medication's importance to people living in sub-Saharan Africa.[14]

In the early 1990s, through a corporate takeover, Aventis acquired Ornidyl. Shortly after, in 1995, they reviewed their new acquisition, noting its high manufacturing costs, poverty in central Africa, and the lack of a market in the wealthy West. Aventis decided there was no profit to be made and stopped producing the drug.

This moment highlights how slippery cure can be. On the surface, the drive to eradicate disease and disorder appears to underpin the development and production of eflornithine. But actually cure's life-saving purpose slips into the background, overshadowed by profit making.[15]

Production of eflornithine only resumed in 2001 after it was also found to successfully remove women's facial hair, not permanently but for eight weeks at a time. Bristol-Myers Squibb and Gillette rebranded the drug Vaniqa and started marketing it to women in the United States. Pharmaceutical companies call this sleight of hand "repurposing a drug." In this case, the corporations involved placed the purpose of Ornidyl alongside the purpose of Vaniqa, prioritizing the latter. They declared the saving of African lives less important than the manipulating of North American women's body-minds.

In a 2001 advertising spread for its newly released drug, Bristol-Myers

Squibb declared, "If the mustache that prevents you from getting close is yours (not his), it may be time for a beauty about-face. Millions of women like yourself battle unwanted facial hair." This spread, published in *Cosmopolitan*, pictures two white women and two Black women, their faces filling the glossy pages, their skin flawless and hairless. We don't even see the entire face of one of the Black women, only her smiling mouth down to her chin. On her smooth upper lip is a tagline shaped like a mustache. It reads, "Now, there's no such thing as too close."[16]

On the other side of this battle against women's facial hair is the promise of heterosexual intimacy. First, like the marketing for skin lighteners, this ad preys on the shame women have about their body-minds. And then it sweet talks them into dreams of hairless skin and greater closeness with their boyfriends and husbands. Smooth skin practically equals heterosexual bliss.

The contrast between Ornidyl and Vaniqa is stark. One saves lives. The other temporarily removes women's facial hair. One wasn't produced for six years. The other warrants a six-page glossy advertisement insert in a major mainstream women's magazine, leveraging sexist-racist beauty standards and reinforcing the notion that women don't, or shouldn't, have facial hair. In prioritizing U.S. women—many of them white and middle-class—Aventis, Bristol-Myers Squibb, and Gillette leave poor, rural, sub-Saharan Africans to die. In this moment, cure's life-saving purpose is trumped by its life-manipulating and life-prioritizing purposes, both of which seamlessly slide into its profit-making purpose.

If left up to the pharmaceutical companies, the story would end here. But today, because of an international activist campaign led by Doctors Without Borders in 2001 and a media exposé of Vaniqa, Aventis (now Sanofi) donates eflornithine to the World Health Organization, which in turn distributes it for free to clinics and doctors in central Africa. For the moment, Ornidyl and Vaniqa exist side by side, the second no longer eclipsing the first, but not because of any structural change inside the medical-industrial complex. Rather Sanofi decided under pressure to make a donation. Long-term access to eflornithine to cure sleeping sickness now relies entirely on the pharmaceutical company's continued goodwill.

....

The life-saving, life-manipulating, life-prioritizing, and profit-making purposes of cure interact in many ways. They bolster, oppose, trump, provide cover for one another. They slip and slide across time and space. These interactions are laden with the politics of race, class, gender, sexuality, and disability. They are bound up with imperialism and multinational capitalism. Through it all, we are urged to believe in the promise of technology as significant as the "resurrection drug" and to desire technology as cosmetic as Vaniqa.

brilliant imperfection

ROLLING

As a walkie, I took a while to learn that when I stroll down a
sidewalk with wheelchair users, I do not need to slow down.[1]
If there are curb cuts at every intersection and the concrete
is relatively smooth, wheelchair users, especially those in
power chairs, can leave me in the dust every time. In truth,
they're slowing down to be with me.

At disability gatherings when manual chair users become
tired or have difficulty with a steep incline, they're not likely
to ask walkies for a push. Rather they'll ask their power
chair–using friends for a hitch, grab a wheelchair handle,
and zip away in a train of two, leaving the walkies far
behind.

I don't mean that rolling is better than walking; just that
walking has long been overrated.

7 AT THE CENTER OF CURE

Carrie Buck I: Yearning

I start with a single photograph.[1] Carrie Buck and her mother, Emma, sit outside the State Colony for Epileptics and Feebleminded in Lynchburg, Virginia. They look into the camera, steely-eyed. The older woman rests her hand on the younger woman's shoulder.

That November day in 1924, Carrie had already been locked up for five months, her mother for four years. I read the histories, track the dates, trace the chronology of events that led to this photo. In 1910 Carrie was taken from her mother and placed in foster care with John and Alice Dobbs. In 1920 Emma was arrested, deemed a low grade moron, and committed to the Colony for supposed sex work. In 1923 John and Alice's nephew Clarence Garland raped Carrie. She became pregnant, and the Dobbs family reacted by declaring her feebleminded. In March 1924 the Virginia state legislature passed the Eugenical Sterilization Act, which made state-mandated and state-coerced sterilization legal. Two months later John and Alice sent Carrie to the same state institution that housed her mother. She was eighteen years old.

Carrie, I keep waiting for the histories to mourn, rage, reach toward you, your body-mind as solid as your mother's hand on your shoulder.

Three years later she landed, a poor white woman, in the U.S. Supreme Court as the judges decided the case *Buck v. Bell*. They declared compulsory sterilization laws constitutional. Fortified by that decision, the state of Virginia sterilized Carrie and only then released her. Emma never got out, dying at the Colony.

I, diagnosed mentally retarded in 1966, imagine, yearn, stretch toward Carrie, judged feebleminded in 1924. So many people have vanished into the whirlpool of history.

I imagine her voice—rough and southern. Imagine her head cocked, how she might tell this story.[2] She says: *The newsmen come 'round now and again. They always want to know if I missed having children. Ask as if that's the only regret they can imagine. Oh, I got plenty of regrets, but kids are only one of many. Least I've not been a live-in for a long time. Swore when me and Billy got married, I'd keep my own house. No more sleeping in the back room of whatever cold-eyed missus I cooked and cleaned for. I liked being Missus Eagle.*

I find reams of information, dozens of portraits, a plentiful record of the eugenicists who engineered the case against Carrie—Albert Priddy and later John Bell (after Priddy's death), Aubrey Strode, and Irving Whitehead. They needed their sterilization law determined constitutional and so went looking for a case to take all the way to the Supreme Court.

The body-mind as gristle
and synapse, water
and bone, pure empty
space, the body-mind
as legal precedent.

I imagine Carrie sucking hard candy at a kitchen table, Formica yellowed and cracking. She keeps talking. *I've seen those pictures. Hell, I sent that bastard Bell my wedding photo when he asked.*[3] *Mr. Bell, he was the big boss man at the Colony. I'd flat out refuse now, but back then Mama still lived up there, and me and Billy dreamed of bringing her to live with us. I thought playing nice with Mr. Bell might help my case. So I sent him that photo of us looking so fine, me grinning up a storm. Billy'd just run his hand through my hair, down my back. That man's fingers could be so shockingly soft. We were silly happy that day. And up they went and cut Billy out of the picture.*[4] *Simply cut the photo in two. Threw out Billy's half. All they wanted was a photo of Carrie Buck for their precious little records. I hated their cameras, their files, their tests. They weren't even tricky, goddamn liars. Back then I thought I could leave all the heartache behind by becoming Missus William Eagle.*

Aubrey Strode prosecuted the court case named after Carrie Buck and wrote the law under which she was sterilized. Irving Whitehead supposedly defended her. But really Colony superintendent and compulsory sterilization proponent Albert Priddy paid Whitehead for his services. And finally John Bell, the Bell in *Buck v. Bell*, was Priddy's successor, wielding the scalpel in Carrie's sterilization. Yes, this was a conspiracy. The histories lavish details upon them, turn Carrie into a shadow, ghost, placeholder.

She talks to me, quiet and intense. *The newsmen never ask 'bout Mama. I hardly knew her before I got to the Colony. I was taken away from her when I was little. Anyway, when I was locked up, my baby girl had just been born.*

Vivian was her name. I could still feel that Dobbs boy, his mean little hands at my throat. I was scared and mad.

That damn place. Food was bad, beds worse, work harder than for Mrs. Dobbs but not by much. If I never scrub another fifty-gallon kettle, ladle out rancid broth, it'll be too soon. The ladies who run the wards could be mean as copperheads or mild as summer colds. When they took a hankering, they'd tie us to our beds, lock us down in the coal bins. But the absolute worst was the boredom, how we'd sweat pure body-numbing blankness every damn day, no relief except to make a scene, then blame some imbecile who couldn't talk.

But those well-funded white men, their body-minds haven't vanished. Their ideas and legacies are alive and well. Charles Davenport masterminded the Eugenics Records Office with its wall upon wall of cabinets full of human pedigrees. Harry Laughlin lobbied for immigration quotas and antimiscegenation laws, wrote a source book called *Eugenical Sterilization in the United States*, and won awards from the Nazis.[5] Arthur Estabrook conducted fieldwork, drew thousands of pedigrees, published dozens of case studies, and testified against Carrie, calling the Buck family a "defective strain."[6]

Eugenicists one and all—they considered some body-minds good, using as their criteria whiteness and wealth, heterosexuality and manhood, U.S. citizenship and Christianity, ablebodiedness and ablemindedness. Other body-minds they deemed bad—marked by defectiveness, degeneracy, deficiency, perversion, feeblemindedness, poverty, criminality, and weakness. They worked to reproduce the "good" and discard the "bad." History is a torrent shaped around them.

> The body-mind a spasm, a
> chance, a near
> miss, fragile as one
> egg, one sperm.

Buck v. Bell landed in the Supreme Court, which is exactly what Aubrey Strode, Irving Whitehead, and all the rest had planned. The white men up on their bench ruled against Carrie, 8 to 1, no surprise. Only Pierce Butler dissented; he left no words for the record. On May 2, 1927, Oliver Wendell Holmes Jr. wrote the majority opinion. History saved his voice for posterity: "We have seen more than once that the public welfare may call upon the best citizens for their lives. It would be strange if it could not call upon those who already sap the strength of the State for these lesser sacrifices . . . in order to prevent our being swamped with incompetence."[7]

I let Carrie's voice ride over Holmes. *Mama and me, we talked every day. We'd sit outside when they'd let us, side by side like that day the court man came. Estabrook was his name. He drew those little pictures he kept calling pedigrees and asked all sorts of stupid questions, making up some fool story 'bout Mama, me, and my baby girl. By the end we were so riled, just glowered at him as he took our picture. I started cussing him out, 'til Mama lay a hand on my shoulder.*

But Holmes didn't stop. He wrote on: "It is better for all the world, if instead of waiting to execute degenerate offspring for crime, or let them starve for their imbecility, society can prevent those who are manifestly unfit from continuing their own kind. . . . Three generations of imbeciles are enough."[8] His words have never been overturned.

Carrie, you of course were one of Oliver's three generations along with your mother and daughter. Sham, trickery, travesty—that case was never about protecting your body-mind. I can almost see the word *imbecile* etched on your belly, each letter a thin line of scar. Trapped, hounded, desperate—you were released only after John Bell cut into you on October 19, 1927.

....

> The body-mind as gut
> and bowel, hope
> and dread,
> literal trash.

Carrie insists, her words becoming their own torrent. *We'd sit outside, and Mama'd tell stories. Uncle Pete learning the fiddle. Cousins I never knew I had. Her loving to swim at dusk. She missed it so much, even after all those years locked up, couldn't bear looking at the James River that run behind that damn place. Hurt her not to be able to slip into the water, feel its current against her skin.*

See, they always shamed us by saying how us feebleminded girls weren't to be trusted. Yeah, I could tell you I wasn't really feebleminded 'til the cows come home, but that'd be a lie. They called all of us in there feebleminded, didn't matter whether a girl was an imbecile, a drunkard, or just plain poor.

I trail the histories from Lynchburg, where Carrie was judged feeble-minded in 1924, to the Fairview Hospital and Training Center, where I was diagnosed retarded in 1966.

Carrie, how many of us become exactly who the doctors and judges, teachers and social workers, scientists and psychiatrists declare us to be?

I want a history that leans into Carrie's voice. She says: *If you weren't a bit funny when they dragged you into that place and you stayed awhile, you sure turned out that way. By the time I got there, Mama was forgetting things, getting bitter quiet. That place changes you bad. I've never been the same.*

Carrie Buck II: Torrent of History

So many records have been mislaid, forged, burned. If it hadn't been for the Supreme Court case, Carrie Buck wouldn't even be a placeholder in the histories. Instead she'd be a number, a lost detail, another poor white woman caught in the grind, locked up in the white-only State Colony for Epileptics and Feebleminded. Two hours due east in Petersburg was the more crowded and less funded Black-only Central State Hospital, called the Central State Lunatic Asylum for Colored Insane until the late 1800s. It housed African Americans deemed insane or feebleminded.[9] I imagine the thousands of Black women and men imprisoned there during the time Carrie was at the Colony in Lynchburg. I need to ask: in what ways did Carrie's whiteness shield her?

> The body-mind as symbol,
> metaphor, academic
> abstraction, the body-mind
> as history.

Carrie's voice, a slow, strong drawl, pulls against the histories. *I got no idea if Priddy or Bell used his knife on Mama. She never said. I just assumed so, but they kept her. If I wanted to leave, Mr. Bell said I'd have to go through the operation. But I didn't want the operation, see. I kicked against it. Still, I was happy to get out of there after he cut me. The bastard. Yeah, I was sad to leave Mama behind. Left hoping to see my baby girl, get off parole, have Mama come live with me.*

Along with the Sterilization Act, the Virginia legislature in 1924 passed the Racial Integrity Act, outlawing mixed-race marriages. As *Buck v. Bell* moved through the legal system, Virginia's head of the Bureau of Vital Statistics, Walter Plecker, an avowed white supremacist and rabid eugenicist, wreaked havoc with that law. He rewrote birth and death certificates, shredded marriage licenses, threatened interracial couples with jail. He made lists, tracked families, knocked on doors.

Carrie, in those Jim Crow years, did you know folks who fled, resisted, caved under Plecker's demands? He pursued Black people; dark-skinned immigrants; poor white women; Chickahominy, Rappahannock, and Monacan families—Indigenous people who he believed were pretending to be white. Hell, Carrie, I wonder if you knew Plecker himself. Did he or his agents knock at your door, joining John Bell and his caseworkers in harassing you and your family?

Obsessed, Plecker wrote thousands of letters, bullying and berating. He didn't care about controlling the sexual behavior of heterosexual white men with their histories of raping Black women. Rather he targeted new mothers, midwives, babies he unabashedly classified as "mongrel." He told one mother, "This child is not allowed to mix with white children. It [this child] cannot go to white schools and can never marry a white person in Virginia. It is a horrible thing."[10] His words have carried through the decades.

The body-mind
as ink on paper:
court order, medical
diagnosis, data
on file.

Carrie's voice reaches me steady, blunt, unwavering. *Mr. and Mrs. Dobbs got to keep Vivian, changed her name to theirs. I didn't even know when she died, eight years old, smart as a whip. That's what I heard when I asked around. I did get off parole, thankfully, lucky me. They were watching all of us Bucks. I mean really watching us. They knew where we lived, who we spent time with, how we put food on the table. They harassed my sister Doris bad. She's younger than me by a couple years. Bell had it out for her. Sent her up to the Colony not long before he let me out. She got the knife too—fourteen years old, still a girl really.*

Later she'd tell the newsmen: "They operated on me for the appendix. They had to do what they did to me when they had me open. I never knew anything about it."[11] *But really we all knew. Some of us just didn't have kids to feed, dress, put to sleep. It was a mercy and a grief. But see, Doris, she wanted babies so bad. Every now and then she'd say to me, "If ever I find me a lawyer man, I'm going to sue the pants off those bastards." We'd laugh, but I knew she was dead serious. Good thing she never went back with her shotgun.*[12]

Walter Plecker and John Bell must have known each other. In 1925 Plecker ranted, "Not a few white women are giving birth to mulatto children. These women are usually feeble-minded, but in some cases they are simply depraved. The segregation or sterilization of feeble-minded females is the only solution to the problem."[13] I imagine John Bell nodding and smiling. They waited, eager for the Supreme Court decision.

Several years later Bell moralized about operating on Carrie: "Sexual delinquency is probably a thing that will have to be contended with for many years, unless she should find a suitable husband, and marry and settle down. . . . [She] has a sister who was also delinquent; they come from a long line of mental defectives." But he ends by bragging that after surgery "she was immediately returned to society and made good."[14] I picture Plecker and Bell jubilant—state-mandated and state-coerced sterilization finally constitutional.

Carrie, history slammed into your body-mind, an unyielding torrent. Did your bruises ever heal? Did you taste the bitter lack of children, those grim institutional years? Or was sex without the risk of pregnancy a complicated thing, an enraged blessing?

The body-mind
a grunt,
a wail,
a gust
of pleasure.

Carrie Buck III: Feebleminded

My imagination of Carrie Buck may simply be a projection of my yearning onto her, but nonetheless she insists, telling me that she's not done. *I never got Mama out. Me and Billy could barely keep a roof over our heads. Billy worked himself to the bone, traveling and digging ditches, mucking out pig pens, repairing barns. He never brought much money home, and for a long time all I got for cleaning was my meals. Still we would've done anything to have Mama here. I wrote to Bell over and over. Really begged him. About a decade before Mama died, I wrote: "Dr. Bell, I would just love to take my mother out for the winter. . . . We will send her the money to come on and I will fix for her if you think she can make the trip alright. I am planning on sending her the money some time in September or October. I don't know for sure when, but as soon as I can get it."*[15] *They might've released her if we could've ever paid her bus ticket.*

I keep reading this unyielding torrent called history. In the last decade the historians have discovered that Carrie wasn't *really* feebleminded; neither was Emma, nor Vivian. They're in an uproar. They repeatedly use Vivian's report card—one A, three Bs, and one C—to prove their discovery.[16] These details have become a revelation. Historian Paul Lombardo calls his recent book *Three Generations, No Imbeciles*. He has uncovered many details, fit this story together in a new way, conclusively establishing *Buck v. Bell* as a sham trial never intended to protect Carrie. But Lombardo and other historians seem surprised that *defective* and *feebleminded* are political fabrications. Ableism locks them into the need to proclaim Emma, Carrie, and Vivian not imbeciles.

So many lives hung on the slippery words *defective* and *feebleminded*. Sex workers, immigrants, people of color, poor white people, people with psychiatric disabilities, people with epilepsy, so-called sexual deviants, blind people, deaf people, physically disabled people, unmarried women who had sex, effeminate men, prisoners, intellectually disabled people were all deemed defective or feebleminded at one time or another. The list kept shifting over the decades, but the meaning of those words stayed the same—inferior, immoral, disposable.

Eugenicists believed feeblemindedness, poverty, and violence to be hereditary—multigenerational defects, menaces that would lead to the downfall of the United States. They sought to cure the nation, restoring its health as defined through nationalism, whiteness, and wealth. More than sixty thousand people were involuntarily sterilized, tens of thousands of people institutionalized, countless immigrants turned away at the border.[17]

Carrie, the recent historians seem to think the court case and your sterilization might have been less a travesty if you had been intellectually disabled. They want to believe in *real* imbeciles. I, diagnosed mentally retarded in 1966, imagine, yearn, stretch toward you, judged feebleminded in 1924.

The body-mind
a live wire
singing fear,
hope, desire.

I feel Carrie's words dappling through me. *I knew Mama's health wasn't good, something 'bout her heart. I didn't get to see her again. Roy (he's my baby brother) and me hitchhiked down to see her after we got more news 'bout her health. She'd already been dead awhile. Buried at that damn place, the number 575 on her gravestone, though I hear tell of a new marker with her whole name, but I've never seen it.*[18]

There's one last photo, taken in 1982, not long before Carrie died. She was seventy-six, living in a rural nursing home for poor people. She stares at this camera too, an old woman looking nothing like her younger self, except for the same steely eyes.[19]

Carrie, doctors waited all over the country for your sterilization to be proclaimed constitutional, that court case slicing through decades of body-minds.

Carrie stays stubborn, unbroken, ready. She says: *They come 'round with their cameras and microphones every once in a while, like I was some famous person or what happened is some fancy story. Sometimes I hear their cars pull up, and I close the curtains. Holler, "Go away. I can't talk."*[20] *There never was a camera I liked but the one on me and Billy's wedding day.*

....

Beyond the histories, I imagine a congress of sterilized women and men
—raging, fierce, grief-filled. Puerto Rican women sit with Appalachian
men. Indigenous teenagers sit with self-described mad women. Disabled
people who have lived their entire lives locked away in state-run hospitals sit with southern Black women who know all too well the words
Mississippi appendectomy, the meaning behind them. Women of color
ordered by judges or paid to take Norplant sit with white women tricked
into signing tubal ligation consent forms. They won't be asking for apol-
ogies or giving absolution, but rather holding remembrance, demanding
reparations, maybe even plotting revolution.

Lives Reduced to Case Files

....

Sometimes all the medical-industrial complex leaves behind are case
files—that scramble of charts, letters, clinical notes, diagnoses, photographs, birth and death certificates, and court orders used to track people's lives through medical care and confinement. In the era before elec-
tronic records, these files reduced countless body-minds to paper and
ink, stored in vaults, drawers, and boxes upon boxes. Now the same reduction happens in bits and bytes, stored on computers.

   These files, whatever form they take, possess power. They document,
prove, and defend treatment and cure. They transform people into diagnoses and "expert opinions." Tellingly they are called case files, not
personal files, personhood itself receding. Thousands of stories vanish
beneath their authority.

i.

I return to Fairview, where staff snapped annual photographs of the
people who lived there—more pieces of documentation to add to their
endless case files. I look at a single photo of a white disabled girl wearing
a polka-dot dress. An information board held in front of her reads: "OFH.

11 FEB 65. DALY, MOLLY JO. CASE NO. 5528. B.D. 5-10-54. EYES—
BLUE. HAIR—BR. WT—61 LBS. HT—50 INS."²¹ Molly Jo was ten years
old; she had been locked up at Fairview for eight years and would remain so
for another twenty-seven, her case file thick with letters, reports, photos.

I watch her brother's documentary *Where's Molly: A True Story of Those
Lost and Found* again. To piece her history together, Jeff Daly uses photographs, including pictures from her case file. I imagine him laying them
out on his kitchen table, sliding the snapshot of Molly and him playing
together on the floor, grinning into the camera, next to the case file photo
of his sister at ten in a polka-dot dress, case number 5528. Jeff pieces ten
years' worth of Fairview photographs together into a collage, chronicling
Molly from ages seven to seventeen. The information board, either held in
front of her or hanging from her neck, marks each one. The dates and mea-
surements change from year to year, but her case number stays the same.

In the documentary, Jeff narrates, "Molly's records show over time
that her behavior worsened. The staff reported that she was bored, agitated, frustrated, and had tantrums." He most likely lifted this information from her case file. I yearn for a different story, not this one written
as case notes by Fairview workers. In another photo we see Molly smile,
a front tooth missing. Jeff's narration keeps unfolding: "In her . . . teens
and early twenties, annual photos show the effects of self-abuse. She
threw herself down and slammed her head on the cement floors."

I want to hold space for Molly beyond this single story that edges into
blaming her for her own abuse. What, pray tell, happened before her
head hit the cement? Was she pushed, thrown, hit? Let my questions be
a pry bar. Was she fighting meds, restraints, some unreasonable rule or
abusive punishment? Was she communicating in the only way available
to her? Let me wrench open this case file that lays claim to the entire
truth. Who do those notes protect with their blameless, sanitized story
of self-abuse? Case files erase so much.

In 1971, six weeks before her seventeenth birthday, another case file
photo shows lumps on Molly's forehead, her skull visibly misshapen. Jeff
continues, leaning into the case file's authority: "She knocked out her
teeth and fractured her skull. She was medicated and restrained." I have
no clue why he would accept this particular telling as true.

Former Fairview resident Terry Schwartz reports such a different reality: "Staff could do anything they wanted to us. . . . They could slap
us. They could hit us. They [could] do anything to us. . . . We [were]

under control of them. They [did] all the thinking for us; they [did] all the talking for us." He remembers staff stuffing him into a laundry bag, which they then hung from a pipe in the ceiling. They left him hanging there for an hour or more. When asked why staff did this, he answers, "They just [did] it to be ornery."[22] I want Jeff to pay close attention to Terry Schwartz's analysis.

At the same time, I know that few remnants remain from Molly's three and a half decades at Fairview. I can feel the stolen years and histories swirling around Jeff—a vast thievery. His search, gleaning what he can from case notes and photos, is a kind of resistance, however incomplete, a brilliant imperfection in the face of erasure.

In the last photo of Jeff's collage, Molly stares, eyes shadowed, nose broad—a mug shot. I imagine her screaming, "Leave me the fuck alone." All I can do is mourn and rage.

ii.

The case files were similarly unending at the Ionia State Hospital for the Criminally Insane, two hours outside of Detroit. In the 1960s and 1970s staff wrote thousands upon thousands of case notes, describing, tracking, demonizing Black men diagnosed with schizophrenia or, as white psychiatrists Walter Bromberg and Frank Simon named it, "protest psychosis."[23] Staff wrote, "[He believes] white men are against [him,] including police officers." They wrote, "[He] supports Black Power." They wrote, "[He] blames the judge's whiteness as his reason for being in jail."[24] Their notes filled reams of paper, pathologizing the sheer naming and resisting of white supremacy. Let my questions again be a pry bar. How much did these men lose, diagnosis justifying their long-term incarceration, confinement posing as treatment and cure?

Thousands of case files from Ionia still exist today. Many are ten, twelve, fourteen inches thick, an onslaught of paper often ending with a death certificate. But the actual people caught in the vice grip that declared them both criminal and insane—they have all but vanished. Ionia State Hospital transformed them into case files; their thoughts, feelings, desires buried in that onslaught.

I imagine their pleasure, their resistance, their regret, their bone-crushing loneliness and lack of privacy. Imagine them filling Ionia's locked wards. Imagine them sneaking cigarette breaks, spending hours scheming escape. Imagine them sleeping and waking and sleeping again, losing all sense of time in the blur of indefinite imprisonment. My imagination becomes a pry bar. Ionia didn't actually transform them into case files. They didn't literally become paper and ink but remained flesh and blood, remained themselves, simply remained. Still, they have all but vanished.

In the decades since Ionia's closure in 1975, those case files have become data, patterns, histories. Researchers use them as an archive, sifting through mounds of documents grown yellow, brittle, musty. The people beneath all that paper disappear again, only to reappear as extrapolations, aggregates, anonymous case studies—each sincerely claiming to be a life story. Let me say again: case files erase so much.

I yearn for the living, breathing people who paced Ionia's halls sedated with Serpasil and Haldol. I mourn for the white women whose only choices were heterosexual marriage and motherhood, diagnosed in the 1940s with paranoid schizophrenia, in the 1950s with "schizophrenia—chronic undifferentiated type," and in the 1960s with "depressive neurosis."[25] I ache for the white gay men deemed violent criminal sexual psychopaths under Michigan's Goodrich Act of 1939.[26] I rage for the overwhelming number of poor and working-class Black men, many of them from Detroit, labeled dangerous and paranoid schizophrenic during the 1960s at the height of fierce political protest. I think again about loss. What did those men's families and communities lose, diagnosis justifying the severing of kin, friends, comrades from each other? What did the Black civil rights and Black Power movements lose, diagnosis undermining their radical calls for justice?

....

Case files will never provide the answers. Instead they tell stories entirely distorted, filtered through diagnosis, treatment, and cure; stories that flatten body-minds onto paper and computer screens, reduced to fit into vaults and servers. They lay claim to the truth. They lie.

Living with *Monkey*

For hundreds of years, white disabled people and people of color—both disabled and nondisabled—have lived with *monkey*. We've faced that taunt, freak show name, scientific and anthropological designation both publicly and privately, in the spotlight and not.

Freak show managers used to print posters proclaiming us the "What-Is-It?," capitalizing on the nineteenth-century uproar about Darwin's theory of evolution and the scientific conviction that a missing link between human and primate had to exist. They used to commission portraits like the one of G. A. Farini holding Krao Farini. She clings—a six-year-old, brown-skinned girl—to the white showman, her legs and arms wrapped around him. He wears a three-piece suit and bow tie while she is entirely naked in order to show off her supposedly hairy legs, arms, and back.[27] He exhibited her as "Ape Girl" and the "Missing Link." Natural historians used to dissect our body-minds after we were dead and display our skulls, skeletons, genitals in museums. Anthropologists used to measure our heads.

Many a naturalist and politician has shared Georges Cuvier's belief that "the negro race . . . manifestly approaches to the monkey tribe. The hordes of which this variety is composed have always remained in a state of complete barbarism."[28] And more than a few journalists, scientists, and doctors have agreed with Carl Vogt when he wrote that "born idiots present as perfect a series from man to the ape as may be wished for. . . . We need only place the skulls of the Negro, chimpanzee and idiot side by side, to show that the idiot holds in every respect an intermediate place between them."[29] Throughout the nineteenth century and beyond, racism, colonialism, and ableism have been coiled together inside the word *monkey*.

Today, anthropologists no longer measure our skulls; instead psychologists quantify and rank our intelligence. Bullies circle us, their taunts reverberating. The world names us *monkey* in a myriad of ways.

....

I'm remembering Ota Benga, a central African, Indigenous man, and the white explorer and Christian missionary who named him a cannibal. Hired to obtain people from Africa for exhibition in the "Pygmy village" at the 1904 World's Fair, Samuel Verner either bribed or bought Benga and eight other young men from the Congo, where they had been living under the brutal colonial rule of King Leopold II. Verner shipped these men to the World's Fair in St. Louis and, like freak show promoters before him, made up outrageous lies and stories. He hyped Benga as a savage, his sharp, pointed teeth highlighted in promotional photos: "Have you seen otabenga's teeth! . . . [He] is a cannibal, the only genuine African cannibal in America today."[30] Right behind *cannibal* hovers *monkey*.[31]

But Verner didn't stop there. He went on to muse about the "Pygmies": "Who and what are they? Are they men, or the highest of apes?"[32] With these words, he joined natural historians, engaging directly in the same debate that made the "What-Is-It?" exhibits so popular. Verner continued, "Have they degenerated from larger men, or are the larger men a development of Pygmy forefathers? These questions arise naturally, and plunge the inquirer at once into the depths of the most heated discussions of this generation."[33] *Monkey* hovers inside these queries too, Verner leveraging that word and concept for profit, entertainment, fame, and science.

From cannibal to ape, Ota Benga was named *monkey* even more literally in 1906. Forced to live for a month in the Bronx Zoo monkey house, he shared a cage with an orangutan named Dohong. The man and ape performed together, wearing matching costumes, pantomiming and goofing with each other—Ota Benga made to seem more primate-like and Dohong more human-like. All the while, humans laughed, jeered, and gawked. The sign on Ota Benga's exhibit read: "The African Pigmy, 'Ota Benga.' Age, 23 years. Height, 4 feet 11 inches. Weight, 103 pounds. Brought from the Kasai River, Congo Free State, South Central Africa, by Dr. Samuel P. Verner. Exhibited each afternoon during September."[34] These words make his situation stunningly clear. Imprisoned in a zoo, he became, to thousands of people, nothing but a curiosity, a specimen, a monkey.

More than a century later I'm reading descriptions of Ota Benga and Dohong's time together in the Bronx Zoo and looking at old photos. In one picture, the human stands bare-chested in a forest holding a chimpanzee on one hip.[35] In another, the orangutan sits in a big wooden chair with a chimpanzee named Polly.[36]

Ota Benga and Dohong, I try to imagine the two of you—a human who had survived intense colonial violence at home only to be found by Verner and shipped to the United States, and an orangutan who had been ripped from the nest he shared with his mother high up in the trees of Southeast Asia. After reading the little I can find about your lives, I feel a helpless sorrow. You haunt me. I picture you depressed and enraged by this place you found yourselves in, bewildered by your odd-looking captors. Were there moments at night, the bars of your cage casting long shadows on the concrete floor, when you curled up together, craving each other's warmth, moments when you became exactly who the natural historians and zookeepers, anthropologists and zoo-goers declared you to be? I ask, knowing that neither you nor history will answer my questions.

....

The brutal consequences of *monkey* arise because that word removes some of us from humanity, placing us among nonhuman animals in the natural world. *Monkey* strengthens racist, ableist, and speciesist hierarchies. Once a person is deemed not human, then all sorts of violence become acceptable.

I refuse to abandon the many people who have been exhibited, studied, written about, photographed, imprisoned as *monkeys*. Refuse to forget the dozens of Black, intellectually disabled men and women who worked as the "What-Is-It?" and the "Missing Link." Refuse to turn away from Krao Farini and Ota Benga, Dohong and Polly.

Let me stay with the poor Black men from rural Alabama who participated in the infamous Tuskegee Syphilis Study, which ran from 1932 to 1972. In photos of these men, their arms and legs are covered with syphilitic sores left untreated. In other pictures, chimpanzees used in laboratory experiments ooze with the same sores.[37] Let me stay with the disabled children at Willowbrook State School, intentionally infected with hepatitis from 1956 to 1971. Let me stay with the men locked up at Holmesburg Prison, used in dermatology experiments from 1951 to 1974. Their body-minds were subjected to acid, radiation, an array of chemicals unknown to them. They received three dollars per experiment and lifetimes of scars and body-mind pain. Being treated as not human—an unfeeling thing, a monkey—is full of risk.[38]

The danger partly centers on the white Western domination of the natural world. Human animals have hunted thousands of nonhuman animals to extinction, or near extinction: egrets for feathered plumes on women's hats, bison for pelts and tongues, whales for oil to grease our machines and meat to feed us and our dogs. In many of these rampages, non-Indigenous people have left bloody carcasses behind, heaps of bones, caring not at all about waste, sustainability, the spiritual connection and interdependence between predator and prey. Nonhuman animals become nothing but grist for greed and capitalism.

By removing white disabled people and people of color—both disabled and not—from humanity, *monkey* puts us in danger just as non-human animals are. Disabled writer and animal rights activist Sunaura Taylor reflects, "What does it mean to be compared to an animal? To be called a 'Monkey Woman'? . . . I find myself wondering why animals exist as such negative points of reference for us. . . . No one wants to be treated like an animal. But how do we treat animals? . . . At the root of the insult in animal comparisons is a discrimination against nonhuman animals themselves."[39] Simply put, the brutal consequences of *monkey* arise because humans treat nonhumans brutally.

....

Monkey is a slow grind of shame, an explosion of hate—racism and ableism compounding each other. I remember again that circle of playmates calling me *monkey*, how my sense of self crumpled. After my father arrived and the bullies scattered, I ran away. Unable to be comforted and unwilling to be near humans, I became *monkey*.

Schizophrenia

....

My relationship to the diagnosis of schizophrenia started with nighttime terrors I couldn't shake. Soon voices filled my head. Plans to kill myself whirled inside me. I walked through the summer of 1992 bewildered, terrified, numb, convinced I had gone crazy.

When strangers on the street ask, "What's wrong with you," I never answer, "I came close to schizophrenia but managed to escape."

....

For many years my body-mind was an abandoned house, windows creaking, wind blowing through the cracks, stone foundation beginning to crumble. I had mastered the fine art of disassociation, surviving unbearable childhood violence only by splitting body-mind from self. I could use the words *rape*, *ritual abuse*, *torture*, but they are only shorthand.

I tell this story because I have questions not about the visceral experiences of hearing voices and seeing visions but about the notion of a biologically based disease called schizophrenia that is treated with body-mind-numbing antipsychotic drugs.

My father would wake me in the middle of the night and take me up into the hills or down to the river. He and his buddies, a little cell of perpetrators, would do the unspeakable with rope and words, fire and fists, water so cold it made my bones tremble. I never knew how to find my way home. Body-mind shattered, piece split from piece, broken. Self leapt into trees, squeezed into rocks, went free fall into the Milky Way. It was the only way to survive. Don't be fooled: it wasn't beautiful, even as I spin pretty images. I simply stayed alive.

I tell this story through a thick veil of shame.

That summer my life fell apart, I lived disembodied in all the ways I had learned so well. The voices in my head became louder and louder; their terror and reason, more real, more true, more persuasive than anything else in my world. I tried to tell my closest friends, tried to create a safety net, tried to stay alive. I came close to failing. One evening I bought and consumed more alcohol and sleeping pills than any single body-mind should be able to survive, crawled into the brush, watched the river meander by, and waited.

My body-mind saved me: I vomited and walked the three miles home. I remember neither act. I only know I did them because I arrived on my front porch, T-shirt and shorts soaked, glasses missing; my housemate and close friend A. took me to the emergency room; and the next morning in the psych ward, I washed dried vomit from my hair.

I tell it remembering that at different times and in different cultures, visions and voices have had different meanings, entirely separate from the diagnosis of schizophrenia and all the accompanying fear, hatred, and stereotypes.

I spent a week on that locked ward. It was a voluntary commitment, but if I hadn't agreed, the psychiatrist who saw me after my stomach had been pumped would probably have committed me anyway. I had no health insurance and earned a bit too much money at my part-time job to be eligible for Medicaid, but I lived in a state that had a fund for indigent inpatient psych care. I hated the food and quickly learned not to tell the whole truth about the voices I kept hearing. I stayed out of seclusion and watched the summer Olympics. I stood by the window for hours, looking at the parking lot nine floors below. I knew I needed the sheer physical safety of a locked ward.

A steady stream of friends came to visit. My friend A. advocated for me every step of the way. I had a college degree, white skin, and marginal employment, all of which worked in my favor. I faked my way through more than one diagnostic exam, counting down from a hundred by sevens, spelling *world* backward, naming the U.S. presidents in order from 1965. I managed to keep my queerness hidden. I made it through with white privilege, a small amount of class privilege, some wits, and a fair amount of luck—locked wards being dangerous places for many people.

I tell it knowing that in this time and place the diagnosis of schizophrenia, along with antipsychotic drugs and stereotypes, profoundly shape the experiences of hearing voices and seeing visions.

Still by day three, the psychiatrist was encouraging me to consider antipsychotic meds. At least she asked without posing overt threats of restraints, seclusion, or forced treatment. No one knew what was happening to me. Was this a one-time psychotic break, the onset of schizophrenia, abuse memories surfacing? I hadn't remembered that cell of perpetrators yet. None of us said *schizophrenia*, but we were all thinking it.

I was terrified and ambivalent about being alive, working to shut the voices—auditory hallucinations as they were called here—out of my head. But mostly I was detached, self hovering outside of skin, sensation muted and distant. I knew something dreadful was happening, something I might not survive. I wanted to fix what felt utterly broken and so took my first dose of Haldol, that drug marketed to psychiatrists in the 1970s as a treatment for Black schizophrenia. One ad leads with the tagline "Assaultive and belligerent" and pictures a caricature of an angry Black man with his left hand balled into a fist. It claims, "Cooperation often begins with HALDOL."[40]

I tell this story searching for ways not to shrink it down to my personal account of pain and survival.

After that first dose, I immediately felt worse than I had in weeks, self floating along the ceiling, body-mind ready to collapse. I went home, started what turned into a decade of talk therapy and bodywork, and didn't fill my prescription.

Four and a half months later I sat in the same psych emergency room processing the paperwork for another voluntary commitment, having spent the prior week under an informal twenty-four-hour-a-day suicide watch made possible by a smallish group of friends. We were exhausted, maxed out, the voices in my head louder and more insistent by the day. We knew the chances of my bolting into the below-freezing winter nights were high, and so together we reluctantly decided that I'd return to the psych ward.

> *I tell it insisting on the racialized and gendered history of schizophrenia, how psychiatrists, judges, and prison wardens have wielded that diagnosis to lock up Black men.*

I sat in the ER, agitated, numb, restraining an urge to pace. In therapy I had been exploring strategies for managing the roaring voices in my head, pursuing the possibility that they were dissociative fallout from severe childhood abuse. But really, I knew almost nothing beyond the feeling that my body-mind was a dangerous, out-of-control, untrustworthy place. After an eternity of questions, the psychiatrist doing my intake told me that if I started taking antipsychotic meds that night, they had a bed for me; otherwise they had no space.

Without a bed on this locked ward, where would I be? My therapist was out of town; my support network was on the verge of collapse; my head was full of voices and suicidal schemes. I started to pace, and suddenly the room was crowded—a half dozen nurses and aides ready to restrain me. My friend A. managed to get us five minutes alone, and I took their deal. Did they write the word *schizophrenia* down? And if not that word, then what? What code from the *Diagnostic and Statistical Manual of Mental Disorders, Third Edition* did they use?

> *I tell it unwilling to shun people labeled schizophrenic.*

I spent almost a year on the antipsychotic drug Navane. Once a month I went to Washtenaw County Community Mental Health (WCCMH) in Ann Arbor because I still had no health insurance. I talked briefly with a different psychiatrist each visit and picked up my free prescription. I slept fourteen, sixteen, eighteen hours a day, going to bed crying and waking up the next morning crying. I dealt with side effects no one bothered to explain, because I was on a so-called subtherapeutic dose. My eyes would roll up in my head, and I wouldn't be able stop looking at the sky, the power lines, the line formed by wall meeting ceiling. For months I believed this behavior to be another sign of my craziness until I mentioned it to a shrink at WCCMH, who shrugged and said it was a common side effect. He wrote me a prescription for Cogentin, which both stopped my eyes from rolling up and made my mouth miserably dry.

I tell it, keenly aware of homelessness, imprisonment, long-term institutionalization, surveillance; of the hundreds—no thousands—of body-mind experiences named as schizophrenia; of the social and material consequences arising from that naming.

I still heard voices. I still schemed suicide. I still hovered outside my body-mind. I went to therapy twice a week and started remembering the cell of perpetrators to which my father belonged, how they operated, and what happened to me there. I have no idea what diagnostic code the WCCMH doctors used. They didn't say the word *schizophrenia*. I stayed alive.

No one tracked me and my meds, surveilling what I took and how often. No one committed me involuntarily. I didn't lose my job or my housing. I narrowly escaped schizophrenia and its consequences.

....

Today I still hear voices and see visions. Not frequently but often enough, my body-mind fills with venomous, seductive words and images, remnants of the violence my father and his buddies perpetrated. The hallucinations arrive, a hurricane of self-destruction. Their return marks danger for me. I wander; I plot suicide; I desperately want to drink myself to oblivion; the voices scream up my throat, out my mouth.

I feel so much kinship with homeless people wrapped in torn cloth, mumbling, chanting, howling to themselves. I give them all my change when they ask, watch their faces twitch, hands tremble, eyes roll up in their heads. I remember Haldol and Navane.

....

Some diagnoses describe a body-mind, and others become a prophesy, a justification, a means of social control.

brilliant imperfection

MYRTLE

In the years after my life fell apart, I created an imaginary
tree where I take myself when I need grounding and safety. I
curl into its hollow trunk, climb to its highest branches, feel
its furrowed bark against my skin. The shiny green leaves,
paler underneath, smell exactly like bay leaves. I fashioned it
after a myrtle tree I used to climb at ages ten, eleven, twelve.
Down in the hayfield below our house, it stood amidst the
grass, alone and sturdy. The trunk divided three feet off the
ground, that crook always my first step into its world.

When I transformed it into an imagined place, I made
it taller, broader, leaves more pungent, branches both
sheltering and shielding. It has helped me through many a
flashback and dissociative fugue.

The last time I visited the river valley where I grew
up, I walked down our old driveway into the hayfield and
stretched my arms around that tree, smell of bay leaf
enveloping me. I was surprised by its size—smaller than my
memory, just big enough to cradle a twelve-year-old.

8   MOVING THROUGH CURE

Choosing Disability

Collectively in the white Western world, we go to such lengths to un-choose disability. We wear seat belts. We don't dive into shallow water. We vaccinate against polio and measles. Certainly these actions are about avoiding death, but our avoidance quickly mashes into the un-choosing of disability. Consider for instance public service announcements and advertisements that warn against unsafe and drunk driving. Many of them use disability as the cautionary tale, showing photos of tragic-appearing teenage boys in wheelchairs. One ad from Utah's "Zero Fatalities" campaign in 2009 reads: "Nothing kills more Utah teens than auto crashes. Not fazed? Okay, how does the thought of spending the rest of your life in a wheelchair grab you? Look, every year far too many Utah teens go from cool to crippled in a blink of an eye."[1] Disability and death are paired together, the first considered a more powerful argument against unsafe driving than the second.

We un-choose disability in hundreds of ways. We condone genetic testing for pregnant people and rarely question the ethics of disability-selective abortion. Some pro-choice activists justify late-term abortions with talk about fetal abnormalities—or in plainer language, disability. We accept as a matter of course that sperm banks screen out donors with a whole host of body-mind conditions considered undesirable, including deafness, alcoholism, cystic fibrosis, depression, and schizophrenia. We walk to end breast cancer, run to end diabetes, bike to end multiple sclerosis, dump ice water on our heads to end ALS. We want to control how, when, and if disability and death appear in our lives.

In 1963 my mother was twenty-six, a newly married working-class student struggling through graduate school. Every day she answered to professors who believed women belonged not in the classroom but at home, tending children. In the spring of that year, she discovered she was pregnant with me. That pregnancy was unplanned. It completely changed the course of her life.

I grew up knowing she desperately didn't want a disabled child. She made that clear in a thousand ways. She was an intensely unhappy mother. Maybe she didn't want *any* children. Yet her grief, guilt, bitterness about my cerebral palsy was so distinct, so personal; at ages ten, eleven, twelve, I believed she didn't want *me*. I may have been right. But for sure, if she could have un-chosen disability, she would have.

....

There are also moments when disability is actively chosen. Prospective foster or adoptive parents fill out agency paperwork requesting a disabled child—or more likely in the language of those bureaucracies, a "special needs" child. Pregnant people decide to keep their fetuses predicted to have Down syndrome. Or they decide against genetic testing altogether, letting the crapshoot of disability run its course unimpeded. Deaf people using alternative insemination to become pregnant seek out deaf sperm donors, wanting to increase their likelihood of having deaf children. Transabled people, sometimes called disability wannabes or amputee wannabes, feel a need to be disabled.[2] Many have sought out surgeons, planned self-amputations, or staged disabling events, manifesting their desire in actual disability. Or, unable to acquire a disability, they use crutches, braces, wheelchairs anyway.

How the world treats people who, in some fashion, choose disability reveals so much. When transabled people come out, putting words to their desire, they most often encounter revulsion, anger, disbelief. The medical-industrial complex pathologizes them, labeling their so-called troubled body-minds with the recently invented Body Identity Integrity Disorder. People who choose to increase the likelihood of having a disabled or deaf child are deemed categorically selfish and immoral. They're accused of burdening their children and sometimes publicly shamed by the media. People who forego genetic testing, deciding not to intervene in the possibility of disability, are seen as vaguely foolish. People who choose against selective abortion after a positive test for a variety of genetic conditions are frequently perceived as downright irresponsible. And people who adopt or foster disabled children—the world treats them as martyrs engaged in charity work. The act of choosing disability in the white Western world is never neutral, simply one choice among many, but rather pathologized, shamed, or sensationalized. In contrast, un-choosing disability is celebrated and framed as a collective imperative.

Beyond this binary of choosing and un-choosing lives the many ways we claim disability and chronic illness. We make peace. We accept. We celebrate. We let go. We find pride. We live with ambiguity. We face mortality. We reject pity and overcoming. We build community and grow accustomed to isolation. We seek interdependence. We turn away from expectations of hyperproductivity. We insist on what we know about our own body-minds. We learn to balance loss and pride. We deal with frustration and pain. I'm loath to define claiming. Sometimes it lives near an active choosing of disability; other times it shares much in common with un-choosing; often it is laced with contradiction.

I know hard-of-hearing people who have thrown their hearing aids away and stopped struggling to be part of the non-deaf world. People who might have been able to walk again after their disabling accidents and chose to become wheelchair users. People who much prefer hearing voices or experiencing emotional highs and lows than managing the impacts and side effects of psychotropic drugs. To many non-deaf people, nondisabled walkies, and people without psych disabilities or psych labels, these choices seem unimaginable. But from the inside, they make all the sense in the world. They pave the way for finding community and connection. They allow for greater and easier mobility. They allow us to be ourselves.

On my forty-fifth birthday a friend writes me, "I'm so glad you were born crippled." She's a queer, disabled, white, working-class activist. We've organized together, sat together, struggled together. The word *crippled* makes me smile. In disability communities, many of us call each other *crip*, practicing the art of refashioning and reclaiming language full of hurt, but typically we veer away from *crippled*; it's too much. My friend uses that riskier word with affection. It contains a whirl of pain and centuries of history. The word *born* settles into me as inconvertible truth: I was indeed born forty-five years ago crippled. But *glad* is her gift to me, both surprise and revelation. *Glad* leans against un-choosing, my mother's dismay, a whole world of devaluing and eradication. *Glad* is more than uppity pride and stubborn resistance. *Glad* is matter-of-fact, unmovable in its conviction that the world needs disabled body-minds. *Glad* is a powerful claiming.

Airports and Cornfields

i.

It's late spring in the San Francisco airport. I walk down a long concourse toward the plane that will take me home. I've been in the Bay Area for a long weekend with three hundred LGBTQ disabled people—queer crips as many of us like to call ourselves. I walk slowly, unable to keep up with the frenzied pace. People stream around me. A white businessman with a rainbow flag sticker on his briefcase hurries past an African American woman and her grandson; a Latino man speaking quiet Spanish into his cell phone stands next to a white teen joking in twangy English with her friends; an Asian American woman pushes her cleaning cart by, stopping to empty the trash can. I know something is missing, but I don't know what. I let my exhaustion and images from the weekend roll over me. Suddenly I realize everyone around me has two arms and two legs. They're walking rather than rolling; speaking with their lips, not their hands, speaking in even, smooth syllables, no stutters or slurs. They have no canes, no crutches, no braces, no ventilators, no face masks, no oxygen tanks, no service dogs. Their faces don't twitch nor their hands flop; they don't rock back and forth. They hold their backs straight, and their smiles aren't lopsided. They move as if their body-minds are separate and independent from the others around them. For a split second, they all look the same.

That fleeting experience of sameness reminds me of monocultures—ecosystems that have been stripped, through human intervention, of a multitude of interdependent beings and replaced by a single species. I think of a wheat field with its orderly rows of one variety of grass, a clearcut forest replanted with one variety of tree.

I know there were many kinds of humans in the San Francisco airport. I was surrounded by differences created through race, language, citizenship, age, class, gender, sexuality, geography, spirituality, nationality, body-mind shape and size, and disability and chronic illness I didn't perceive. Yet, even with my recognition of human diversity, that moment at the airport when everyone looked the same has stayed with me.

ii.

It's early autumn, and I step into an agribusiness cornfield. Rows envelop me, the whole world a forest of corn beginning to turn brown. Leaves and husks rattle overhead. I walk along the furrows between rows, step onto the mounds upon which the stalks grow. A repetition of the same plant fills the space. Nothing chirps or rasps, squawks or buzzes; the cicadas and grasshoppers have gone dormant for the season. I see no traces of grouse, pheasant, fox. If it were a rainy day, I'd see brown water running down the slight slope I'm standing on, washing the dirt away before my very eyes.

....

In a monoculture, a world of damage lies beneath the obvious sameness. During that autumn walk, I couldn't smell the pesticide residue, but it hung in the air I was breathing. I couldn't see the petroleum-based fertilizers in the dirt, but they were present in large quantities. I didn't know how depleted the earth was, each corn stalk sucking nutrients from the soil and giving nothing in return. Nor did I notice the six or seven inches of topsoil that had already been washed away in the last hundred and fifty years. I had no visceral awareness of all the invasive pests—the true armyworm, the European corn borer, the corn rootworm, among many others—that breed and eat with abandon in monoculture cornfields, which in turn force agribusiness farmers to spray endless rounds of pesticides.

Simply put, monocultures do an immense amount of damage. So much labor and violence goes into creating and maintaining them. Their existence requires hundreds of eradications and removals.[3]

....

The history of agribusiness corn, soybeans, wheat, and beef haunts me. I return to an old black-and-white photo, scratched and faded at the edges, taken in the 1870s.[4] It starkly portrays the violence on which these monocultures were created. At the center looms a mountain of bison skulls—thousands upon thousands heaped on top of each other, maybe as many as 180,000. No single skull is distinct; instead they blur together, becoming a geometric pattern of bone. Soon they will be ground into fertilizer. Amidst these bones are two men. Both wear dark suits, and each stands with a foot resting on a skull that's been pulled out of the jumble. One is posed at the base of the pile; the other, twenty-five feet above him on top of the mountain. They make me shiver. They are braggarts—maybe bison hunters or government officials or land speculators. Their body-mind language proclaims, "Look, look at what I own."

My heart breaks and breaks again. Starting in the early 1800s, white hunters killed these big shaggy creatures indiscriminately, thirty million in less than a century. They left the carcasses to rot, took only tongues and skins with them to sell. Later white homesteaders collected the bones for fertilizer. The U.S. government encouraged this slaughter as one strategy among many to conquer the Indigenous peoples of the Great Plains. The Lakota medicine man John (Fire) Lame Deer (Lakota) described the connection between his nation and bison: "The buffalo was part of us, his flesh and blood being absorbed by us until it became our flesh and blood. Our clothing, our tipis, everything we needed for life came from the buffalo's body. It was hard to say where the animal ended and the man began."[5] So when, in 1867, Colonel Richard Irving Dodge commanded, "Kill every buffalo you can! Every buffalo dead is an Indian gone," he was calling for genocide.[6] Native peoples were starved, brutalized, killed, driven onto reservations.

White colonial settlers claimed the land as their own, dividing it into neat rectangles, fencing it, and establishing herds of cattle. The near eradication of the prairies started here. The grazing and migration patterns of bison had been integral parts of these ecosystems, whereas cows destroyed the grasses, giving nothing back. And then white farmers literally tore up the prairie with their plows. They planted monocultures of wheat, corn, and soybean. One hundred seventy million acres of tallgrass prairie used to exist in North America; seven million are left now. Today when we eat corn or steak produced on agribusiness farms in the Great Plains, we are connected all the way back to that mountain of skulls. Monocultures start with violence, removal, and eradication.

iii.

The shadows, legacies, and ongoing realities of environmental destruction and genocide, incarceration and involuntary sterilization rise up.

They haunt me. The desire for eradication runs so deep. It is revealed in specific moments, places, and histories—in a fleeting experience of sameness at the San Francisco airport, in an agribusiness cornfield before it's mowed for the winter, in a hundred-and-forty-year-old photo of a mountain of bison skulls. But the desire for eradication is also a pattern reaching across time and space. The un-choosing of disability fits into this pattern, one force among many, threatening to create a human monoculture.

Interdependence

Leaves to stones, earthworms to grizzly bears, prairie grasses to bison—life is connected to life.

I'm at a crip dance. We lean into each other—hands on waists, hands on hips, hands on metal and wood and wheels, canes waving in the air, crutches stomping out the beat. We slide in and through pain, shimmy and strut. We dance with our tongues, our eyes, our sip-and-puff wheelchairs. We dance lying on the floor. We dance into tremors and spasms, through anxiety, inside hallucinations. We take breaks, stretch our backs, our legs, our shoulders. We dance all night.

No single part of an ecosystem can be changed without changing every other part.

I'm at a crip gathering. A woman smoking pot as pain management and a woman with environmental illness made sick by marijuana smoke end up rooming next door to each other, an arrangement that doesn't work at all. We reorganize who is sleeping where to create more access for both of them. We sit with people having seizures, monitor their breathing, keep the space around them as safe as possible. We don't call 9-1-1. We figure out food together. Fragrance-free shampoo and shower chairs in gender-neutral restrooms are the norm.

If we spray DDT to eradicate mosquitos, bald eagle and condor eggs become too fragile to hatch.

I remember all the times I've talked friends and lovers through panic attacks and flashbacks; sat with them during nighttime terrors; brought them tea, Rescue Remedy, or Klonopin, depending on their preferences. All the times they've done the same for me.

If we burn coal to light our homes and power our computers, the air we breathe becomes toxic.

I stay overnight with a friend. She lives in a big, collective house. In the morning I putter around the kitchen. I can tell crips live here. There are straws in the silverware drawer, a sign on the refrigerator reminding people to keep the pantry peanut-free, and ice packs galore in the freezer. From the next room, I hear my friend L., a white, power-chair-using, self-described femmegimp, talking with her care shifter (the person helping her with her morning routine). They're exchanging first-date stories, L. buoying the confidence of the care shifter with tips, jokes, and appreciation. Their stories are interrupted by logistics—which scarf L. wants to wear, what eye shadow will match, when paratransit is coming.

....

The interdependent relationships between disabled people and the people who provide care for us are often messy and fraught with power imbalances rooted in racism, sexism, homophobia, transphobia, ableism, and capitalism. These imbalances frequently cause abuse and neglect for the person receiving care, low wages and exploited labor for the person providing care, and harassment flying in multiple directions. And yet interdependence exists whether it's laced with easy banter and mutuality or with struggle, hierarchy, and exploitation.

White Western culture goes to extraordinary lengths to deny the vital relationships between water and stone, plant and animal, human and nonhuman, as well as the utter reliance of human upon human. Within this culture of denial, when those of us who don't currently need help dressing ourselves or going to the bathroom try to imagine interdependence, we fail. In conjuring a world where we need care to get up in the morning and go to bed at night, we picture an overwhelming dependency, a terrifying loss of privacy and dignity. We don't pause to notice that our fears reflect not the truth but the limits of our imagination.

....

Part of claiming disability is choosing this messy, imperfect work-in-progress called interdependence.

Wanting a Flat Chest

I thought I understood self-acceptance and love—definitely not a simple practice but nonetheless guided by a certain set of principles—until my gendered and sexed self started speaking. When I listened, I discovered an unshakable desire to reshape my body-mind using medical technology—first with chest reconstruction surgery and later with hormone replacement therapy.

All of our body-minds are in motion from the moment of birth to the moment of death. Ask anyone in the throes of puberty or old age. Ask the U.S. soldier back from Afghanistan, dealing with a recent traumatic brain injury; the Afghan civilian whose leg has been shattered in a bomb attack. Ask the person who has lost or gained a hundred pounds; the woman leaving her fifteen-year heterosexual marriage because she's fallen head over heels in love with another woman. Ask the family who over three or four generations climbs out of poverty, maybe through luck or white privilege, education or marrying up.

I remember the last time I went flat chested and bare skinned, age nine camping with my family in Idaho. Dusk licked my ribs, sternum, collarbone. My mother ordered me to put a T-shirt on, right then and there. I protested, "But why, Dad gets to go without a shirt?" Of course, there was no real answer, only a "because."

Our body-minds tumble, shift, ease their way through space and time, never static. Gender transition in its many forms is simply another kind of motion. I lived in a body-mind assigned female at birth and made peace with it as a girl, a tomboy, a dyke, a queer woman, a butch. But uncovering my desire to transition—to live as a genderqueer, a female-to-male transgender person, a white guy—challenged everything I thought I knew about self-acceptance and love.

I am the girl whose breasts develop slowly—fourteen and still not needing the training bra my mother bought me for Christmas. I feel impatient, embarrassed, disconnected from the girls in my school who whisper about their boyfriends and show off in the locker room. But when my breasts do grow, changing the shape of my body-mind in a matter of months, I'm utterly dismayed. I hate the attention my mother pays me.

During this time and place in history, doctors have the authority to name and classify sex and gender, just as they do disability. At the very moment we take our first full-bodied breath, wailing into the world, they declare "boy" or "girl." When that decision doesn't come easily, when a baby emerges with genitals that don't match what they typically associate with male or female body-minds, they make the birth a medical emergency. They diagnose the newborn with one of the many conditions that falls under the umbrella of disorders of sex differentiation. And then they often perform infant genital surgery to create a penis or vulva that more closely matches their vision of boy or girl. Most of these surgeries are not medically necessary, but rather cosmetic, blatantly enforcing what is normal and cutting away that which is declared abnormal.[7]

After my birth, a nurse laid me in an incubator and gave me antibiotics through a tiny IV drip, no one touching me except to turn me under the heat lamp. But before that, the doctors declared me a girl, just as they would name me mentally retarded two and a half years later, confident in their authority to categorize body-minds.

I am the tomboy who spends the summer between my sophomore and junior years of high school working in the woods with twenty other teenagers. We wear blue chambray work shirts with the Youth Conservation Corps logo embroidered on them. I often layer a T-shirt underneath but forgo a bra. My choice of undergarments is obvious and worries the other girls on my crew. They bully and lecture me all summer. I shrug them off, but one of the crew leaders, a twenty-three-year-old hippie guy, starts asking me pointedly why I don't wear a bra. His eyes rake my body-mind.

Decades later, I discovered that I wanted a flat chest. Arriving at that desire, and then accepting it, took a long time. My body-mind politics told me that plastic surgery, particularly for cosmetic reasons, was bad, a tool of the patriarchy, enforcing sexist and racist standards of beauty, encouraging body-mind mutilation and hatred. I thought about rich, white, cisgender women and nose jobs, tummy tucks, and breast enlargements. I thought about upper-middle-class families spending thousands of dollars on synthetic growth hormones in hopes that their short sons might grow up to be tall men. I thought about poor people who can't get the most basic of health care. During her pregnancy with me, my mother had no health insurance, received almost no prenatal care, and so the ovarian cyst that grew alongside me wasn't detected until the crisis of my birth.

I am the dyke whose breasts hang loose under one layer of cloth. I live at a women's peace camp and rage against sexism and men. Many of us go topless, relishing the feel of sun, wind, water on our skin.

Plastic surgeons make so much profit from people who want to change the appearance of their body-minds. Certainly the doctors specializing in double-incision mastectomies and phalloplasties, facial feminization and tracheal shave surgeries, oophorectomies and vaginoplasties become millionaires off of transsexuality and trans people who want and can afford surgery to change our sexed and gendered selves. My politics argued that I needed to change the world and claim my body-mind as it was.

I am the stone butch who traces my lovers' breasts. I lavish them with my fingertips, tongue, tremoring touch. Learn how to bite, pinch, suck, drawing our heat to the surface. Yet when my lovers reach toward my breasts, I can't feel their hands on me.

Gender Identity Disorder

My relationships with mental retardation, cerebral palsy, schizophrenia, and gender identity disorder (GID) range widely. The first of these diagnoses has fallen by the wayside, even as it still stalks me in the form of hate speech. The second found me during my parents' search for a cure and is convenient shorthand when I request disability access, navigate the medical-industrial complex, or deal with random curiosity, but it has never orchestrated a life-changing revelation. The third I narrowly escaped, grateful not because seeing visions and hearing voices are inherently bad or wrong, even when they create havoc, but because the medical treatment and social conditions accompanying that diagnosis are often dreadful. But the fourth, I actively sought out.

I started my search not because I needed a diagnosis for my gender-queer self, nor because I thought of my desire to reshape my gendered and sexed body-mind as a disorder. Instead I wanted chest reconstruction surgery, and in turn my surgeon wanted a letter of recommendation from a therapist confirming that I had GID and was a good candidate for surgery. In the scheme of providing medical technology for gender transition in 2002, this surgeon was neither conservative nor liberal. According to the 2001 Standards of Care created by the Harry Benjamin International Gender Dysphoria Association, he could have asked for much more or much less.[8] He might have operated without a letter, but he clearly wanted one.

....

Like diagnoses in general, GID can be thought of as a static category that describes a specific body-mind condition and directs a course of treatment. Or it can be thought of as a tool embedded in time, space, culture, and science. In 2002 GID lived in the *Diagnostic and Statistical Manual of Mental Disorders, Fourth Edition, Text Revision* (DSM-IV-TR) and is traceable over the decades.

One strand of this history starts with the first edition of the DSM in 1952. The body-mind experiences of trans and gender-nonconforming people were placed in the overarching category "Sexual Deviations," which included homosexuality, transvestism, pedophilia, fetishism, and sexual sadism. From there, the diagnosis that became known in 1994 as GID twisted and turned through four editions of the DSM. In 1980, as lesbian, gay, and bisexual identities and experiences were being removed from the DSM-III, "Sexual Deviations" became "Paraphilias," and "Transvestism" became "Transvestic Fetishism." Transness also appeared in two other diagnoses: "Transsexualism," used for adults and adolescents, and "Gender Identity Disorder of Childhood." The 1987 revision of the DSM-III added "Gender Identity Disorder of Adolescence and Adulthood, non-transsexual type" to this convoluted heap of diagnoses. The 1994 DSM-IV combined most of these diagnoses into "Gender Identity Disorder," with one symptom list for adults and another for youth. "Transvestic Fetishism" remained the same.[9]

At this point, my head is spinning. The criteria for each diagnosis keep shifting; the lines between categories blur. The words *disorder, paraphilia, fetish* echo through the maze; shame, violence, and hatred follow close behind. There is nothing neutral about the DSM.

....

My search for a GID diagnosis started with the *DSM-IV-TR*. In 2002 the most conventional treatment, laid out in the Standards of Care, began with three months of psychotherapy, which led to hormone replacement therapy and then to any one of a number of surgeries, including chest reconstruction.[10] After finding a surgeon who didn't require hormones before surgery, I started looking for a therapist who had the same philosophy and didn't require three months of therapy, partly because none of this health care was covered by insurance. I found a social worker through word of mouth in the local trans community. She wanted five sessions.

She posed a lot of questions—a few of them insightful, many of them irrelevant, and several of them directly offensive. I vividly remember the moment when she asked, "Was your father a cross-dresser; did he have any sexual fetishes or perversions?" She didn't inquire about my mother; evidently her behavior was inconsequential. I paused. The ironies overwhelmed me. To my knowledge, my father wasn't a cross-dresser, but I certainly was, wearing his work clothes throughout my teenage years. I adored the faded blue denim jeans and flannel shirts he handed down to me, even as my mother hated seeing me, her eldest crippled daughter, dressed in his clothes. But he was also a child molester, a pedophile in the language of the *DSM*. That reality shaped my entire childhood. I would have far preferred a cross-dressing father.

These inappropriate questions about my father were made appropriate by the *DSM-IV*. The diagnosis GID lived next to "Transvestic Fetishism," which was placed next to "Pedophilia," the latter two lumped together as "Paraphilias" and all three listed in the same chapter. Within this scheme, my therapist's questions made clinical sense. In other words, the taxonomic structure of the *DSM* shaped her understanding of GID, my father, and me.

At the end of our five sessions, I received the letter and diagnosis I needed. I was able to navigate the whole process with my sense of self intact, because I had a community network, I was familiar with the routine of therapy, and I knew just how honest to be.

....

But wait, the maze isn't finished. The *DSM-IV* has become the *DSM-5*, and GID is now gender dysphoria (GD), focused not on trans people's gender identities per se but rather on the distress those identities may cause us. This new diagnosis now has its own chapter rather than being grouped with "Sexual and Gender Identity Disorders." At the same time, "Transvestic Fetishism" has become "Transvestic Disorder," complete with an expanded criteria list, remaining grouped with "Sexual Dysfunctions." The move from GID to GD didn't simply happen but resulted from trans activists putting significant pressure on the working groups that created the DSM-5.[11]

In exploring this maze, I'm struck by how much the DSM has changed over time. These transformations underline how intensely diagnoses are made up. There is nothing inevitable, natural, or inherent about GID or GD. They are fabricated categories that reflect current white Western cultural and scientific beliefs and practices. Academics call this idea social construction, but I believe the blunter phrase *made up* reveals more about the relationship between diagnoses and the body-minds they categorize. Simply put, the DSM is a highly constructed projection placed on top of particular body-mind experiences in order to label, organize, and make meaning of them from within a specific worldview.

....

Many trans activists pose fundamental challenges to GID and GD. We want to know why these diagnoses live in the DSM. We object to the ways in which the medical-industrial complex defines our genders as disordered. We resist the pathology foisted on us.

And yet I want us to reach farther: to imagine dismantling the DSM itself, discarding the concepts of *disorder* and *defect,* and developing other means of accessing medical technology beyond white Western diagnosis. Yes, I am suggesting a rebellion.

Claiming Ourselves

....

Gloria, every time I see the Foundation for a Better Life billboard of Whoopi Goldberg overcoming dyslexia, I think of you in 1959, a six-year-old girl called stupid by her teachers and held back in the first grade.[12] You taught yourself to write by turning over a sheet of big block alphabet letters and tracing them backward, the lines and curves finally coming into focus. You strained your way through public school, nourished and embattled long before Individualized Education Plans and the Americans with Disabilities Act. You narrowly escaped special ed. I imagine you in the mid-1970s at college on a rich white campus not so far from the poor Black neighborhood where you grew up.

In the years we knew each other, you never stopped wondering how you escaped the gut-aching poverty of your childhood, landing in college, the first and only one in your family to graduate. You watched your brothers and sisters struggle with drugs and alcohol, unplanned pregnancies, senseless arrests. Your escape haunted you.

I remember us watching *Whoopi Goldberg: Live on Broadway* on VHS, shortly after it was released, sitting in your apartment, a bowl of popcorn between us, the VCR whirring away.[13] Whoopi Goldberg was brilliant, shape-shifting from Black man junkie visiting Anne Frank's house to white surfer teen getting an illegal abortion, from a young Black girl wishing for long, straight, blonde hair to a physically disabled Black woman planning her wedding. We laughed, fell silent, talked about those stories of survival and violence for days. But you never connected your dyslexia to Whoopi Goldberg's.

You worked hard not to overcome dyslexia but to get an education and a steady job after you graduated, to keep it in spite of a doubting, hostile boss, to stay safe and strong amidst daily harassment. You wrote and studied for years, becoming a poet and public health nurse. You proved yourself over and over again, never asking for disability access even as reading and writing remained slow, deliberate acts, never naming your dyslexia a disability. There are so many reasons why people don't identify themselves as disabled. Might you have adopted that word if you had known some disabled women of color? If the disability rights movement had been less white?[14]

You and I built our relationship on stories. We sat in movie theaters and pizza joints, poetry readings and creative writing workshops, sat for hour upon hour talking about our lives, listening hard, laughing harder. Our relationship hovered between first date and articulated passion, both of us newly out as lesbians. I was full of fear, longing, an inability to open my body-mind to another human being, and you were struggling to reconcile your queerness with your Baptist family and church, the God who had sustained you through so much.

You wrote me in half a love poem:

We've taken each other
to the attic of ourselves
one continuous speaking
vision. . . .

When we first met, I had recently arrived in the city that was your home,
a young disabled queer fleeing the backwoods of Oregon, gulping down
new ways of thinking, new ways of being. We told stories as if we believed words alone could bridge the chasm between your thirty and my
twenty, your Black and my white, your urban and my rural. I remember
you, me, our one continuous speaking vision with so much gratitude
and tenderness.

You told me about your dyslexia—about teaching yourself to write,
the misery of school, your frequent struggles to read maps. You named
your shame and hurt but never connected those experiences to disability. In our relationship, I was the disabled one.

I told you stories that now thirty years later I've repeated dozens of
times: being called *retard* and *monkey*, struggling to keep up in school,
my slow, slurred speech not being understood, strangers gawking unabashedly. But back then, saying those words out loud was brand new.
I could reveal those moments for the first time precisely because you
listened through your own lived experiences of dyslexia and ableism.

But there are other disability stories I didn't tell then, can barely tell
now: stories about hearing voices and seeing visions, about psych hos-
pitalizations and being housebound for weeks in order to stay alive. I'm
loath to talk about the times I've had to flee queer public space, triggered
by some expression of kinky sex or description of violence, a performance or conversation, slipping out of my body-mind into the past. I
don't tell these stories because they're mired in shame; because I don't
want them to be true; because unlike my tremoring hands, I can hide
these experiences most of the time; because I'd rather not claim that
kind of disability.

Writer and performer Leah Lakshmi Piepzna-Samarasinha reflects
on the twine of gender, race, sexuality, and disability: "Queer women
of color . . . do not want any more identities than we already have to
wrestle with. Our bodies are already seen as tough, monster, angry, seductive, incompetent. How can we admit [the] weakness, vulnerability,
interdependence [of disability] and still keep our jobs, our perch on the

'thin edge of barbwire' we live on?"[15] What did you claim and hide? What did I?

Gloria, my questions make me want to return to our one continuous speaking vision. I remember the few times we danced together—body-minds awkward, unable to find our rhythm. But our stories knew exactly how to waver and flex, slur and limp, burst in jagged letters across the dance floor. This time, through the cracks and across the chasms, we might claim disability together as strength and vulnerability, interdependence and hard work, risk and fear. Claim, as white, disabled, lesbian poet Laura Hershey writes, "our beautiful crip bodies, broken or bent, and whole."[16] Claim ourselves as common as morning coffee.

DRAG QUEEN

Years before transition, I'm at a drag queen extravaganza in Detroit. The queens work the runway, lip-synching Donna Summers, Mary Chapin Carpenter, Gloria Gaynor. They sashay and croon; make us laugh, dance, and swoon. I'm dressed up—satin-backed vest, sharply pressed trousers, hair freshly buzzed. I sit with my dyke friends. We tip the queens with singles slid into stockings and bustiers.

On our way back into the bar after a break, I hold the door for my favorite of the queens, my shaky butchness on full display. She thanks me, and I compliment her glittering gold pumps. In the moment after I've spoken, I watch her recognize me not as a sixteen-year-old boy but a thirty-year-old butch. She gives a little shake, startled. In that split second, I can almost see her later after the show has finished, taking off her wig and dressing to go home. And then we're back here, a young disabled man and a glamorous queen. It's almost enough.

9 IMPACTS OF CURE

Endless Questions

....

what's your defect
where you from
are you a girl or a boy

Strangers, doctors, would-be lovers ask these questions at bus stops and in exam rooms, on first dates and in grocery store aisles. Inside their queries live unchecked curiosity, a barrage of stereotypes, and their need to locate us on diagnostic maps, racial and ethnic maps, gender maps.

....

Every time someone asks me a curious question about my disability, trying to locate my body-mind, and I answer straight up with the words *cerebral palsy*, I affirm the authority of diagnosis to name and describe our visceral realities.

....

can I touch your hair
have you had the surgery
what's wrong with you

On those maps, our lives become mere landmarks. Prurient curiosity takes the place of courtesy, respect, connection. Tellingly, the parallel questions don't exist. In the U.S. no one asks: "What caused your heterosexuality?" "How do you know you're a cisgender man?" "What's wrong with your symmetrical legs that hold you upright and carry you nearly everywhere?" "Why are you healthy all the time?" "You look so white and American: where are you from; can I touch your straight blonde hair?" The endless questions and their exhausting demands only target those of us deemed abnormal and exotic.

People who are white, heterosexual, cisgender, men, middle- and upper-class, Christian, English-speaking, slender, gender-conforming, nondisabled, documented citizens escape these endless questions. According to the logic of privilege, they don't need to be located.

do you have a penis
what happened to you
what's your accent

....

In those exhausting exchanges, my two-word diagnostic answer communicates almost nothing about my body-mind. I think about people with cerebral palsy—friends, acquaintances, poets, singers, comedians, painters, lawyers, activists, bloggers, policy wonks, teachers. We shake, slur our words, drool. We stumble, trip, fall. We lack fine motor coordination. Some of us have hands that curl tightly, muscles locked into contractures. Others of us have hands that flop loosely. We are wheelchair-using quads, crutch-wielding gimps, walkies with slight wobbles in our legs. We use assistive communication technology. Our speech flails and spasms. Our words emerge in breathy whispers. Our voices are fluid and smooth. Really, what do the curious strangers imagine they have learned about me through this single diagnosis?

....

I wish we could turn these endless questions into an angry, righteous, unforgettable poem, a piercing chorus. Maybe then they wouldn't exhaust us.

Ashley's Father
....

Let me say it straight up: I'm furious with the man known in the media only as the father of a disabled girl he calls Ashley. He says she has the consciousness of a three-month-old. In 2004 he and Ashley's mother chose a surgeon to lift her six-year-old uterus out of her body-mind, another doctor to slice her breast buds away, and an endocrinologist to flood her with estrogen. The ethics committee at the Seattle Children's Hospital supported their decisions. Together these procedures functioned to keep their daughter's body-mind small and childlike as she aged, stopping the typical developmental curve from girlhood through puberty to womanhood. He calls Ashley his "pillow angel."[1]

But I want to step away from my fury for a moment because I have genuine questions for you about love. You claim that the love you feel for your daughter motivated all the medical choices you and your wife made. Let me try, just for a moment, to trust your love and engage with you on your terms.

They wanted to protect Ashley from the discomfort of menstruation and large breasts, the harm of sexual assault, and the risk of pregnancy. They wanted her to stay small in order to take care of her more easily. They wanted, in other words, to keep her safe and happy. At the same time, they lack a shared language or communication system with their daughter and believe her to be permanently incapable of making decisions. So they made these life-changing medical choices for her, driven, Ashley's father claims, by love.

But because love has been marshaled repeatedly over the centuries to justify violence heaped upon violence, I'm unwilling to simply accept your claim. Tell me: Is it love when, in the name of nurturing and protecting your disabled daughter, you sterilize her and assure that she will never menstruate or grow breasts?

I know women who can only move one finger; women who operate their wheelchairs by sipping and puffing; women who get lifted to and from the toilet, shower, bed; women who never leave their beds; women who speak with computers or alphabet boards or not at all; women who lost their words at age seventy; women who never had words; women who as girls were thought to be without communication. Busty women, bleeding women, women—all disabled—who are safe, comfortable, and happy.

Tell me: is it love when you reshape your disabled daughter's body-mind so that she will stay small and childlike? I'm having trouble trusting your love.

He believes she has the emotions, psyche, spirit, selfhood of a three-month-old and therefore can never become a woman. In a 2015 interview just before or after Ashley's eighteenth birthday, he wrote: "Physically, without [the medical procedures] she would in all probability have matured into the typical body of a grown female human. However, her cognitive level would never enable her to become a woman. She profoundly and permanently lacks the intellect, agency, decision making, and all other mental aspects of womanhood due to her infant's brain."[2]

She has a condition named with some long Latinate word I can't wrap my slurring tongue around. I recently learned that her disability is also known as cerebral palsy, which means she and I faced the same crapshoot at birth. Her father claims that the medical treatments Ashley underwent are intended only for profoundly disabled children. He believes that people with less significant disabilities shouldn't be fearful or outraged. He wants those of us who walk or roll; who possess language, words, the means to communicate about abstract concepts; who are deemed competent to make decisions about our own body-minds to know that we're not at risk. He thinks he's reassuring us.

Tell me: is it love when you quantify your disabled daughter's selfhood, taking the liberty of defining what a woman's consciousness is? I picture Terri Schiavo lying in her hospital bed. Would you have declared her no longer a woman?

He can argue as much as he wants, but I see my body-mind in Ashley—in her tense, wiry arms and wide grin. I see her crip beauty. The difference between her and me is slight, a simple matter of which brain cells died at birth. I've not been able to read the news stories, medical articles, opinion pieces. Her story is too close. I could have easily joined Ashley in being a "pillow angel."

I must tell you: those two words—pillow angel—bring me to a full stop. Paired together, they are a brick wall. A pillow is a soft cushion; an angel, a sweet, spiritual being filled with innocence. What, then, a pillow angel? I imagine Ashley as a cushion giving you comfort, a cherub resting passively among pillows, a spiritual abstraction. Does love mean denying your daughter's earthbound, everyday, messy body-mind? Do you love her angry, ornery, profane self too?

He names not only his daughter a *pillow angel* but also other significantly disabled children like her. He uses those two words in his interviews and on his website to refer to a whole group of people, leveraging deeply ingrained associations between disability, whiteness, innocence, passivity, and blessing.

I know you intend pillow angel *as an expression of love, but I feel those words in my bones as separation, exclusion, a denial of humanity, almost hate. Could Ashley simply be a disabled girl without words and the means to grasp the decisions you and her mother made about her body-mind—not passive, not angelic, not a blessing?*

Through all his love, he so fiercely protects his anonymity, claiming no identity except as Ashley's father. On his website, he's posted many photos of himself and his family. In one from 2006, they pose in front of the fireplace next to a Christmas tree. His wife, Ashley, and his other daughter are dressed in red; the two girls wear matching outfits. Ashley sits on his lap, his arms clasped around her as she smiles into the camera, eyes bright, body-mind wiry, chin tilted up slightly. She looks ready for mischief.[3]

Really, you all are the picture-perfect white, heterosexual family except for one thing: black bars cover everyone's eyes except Ashley's. I imagine you made this choice in order to protect your privacy as you go about explaining and promoting the set of medical procedures your daughter underwent. But what about her privacy?

The reversal stuns me. For well over a century, disabled people, fat people, intersex people, people with facial distinctions, and people of color have lived among the pages of medical textbooks. They have posed naked, or nearly so, against blank backgrounds, the resulting images captioned with various medical jargon, black bars positioned to cover their eyes. The medical-industrial complex claims these photos as necessary teaching tools, arguing that the black bars protect the subject's anonymity. But I agree with activist Cheryl Chase when she declares, "The black rectangle over the eyes accomplishes only one thing; it saves the viewer from having to endure the gaze of the subject."[4]

In this Christmas photo, the black bar—that bleak interruption of a face, which serves to spotlight the rest of the body-mind—is for once placed on nondisabled, rather than disabled, people. Yet in this context the bars actually serve to draw attention to Ashley, revealing her body-mind even more. I, for one, am happy to see her wide smile. The familiarity of her bent wrists and taut neck catches me.

Is it love when you protect your privacy while displaying your daughter on the web and in the media? Love braids itself with the desire to protect. You express that yearning repeatedly—wanting to shield Ashley from discomfort, abusive care, and potential institutionalization. But protecting her privacy isn't high on your priority list. It makes me suspicious of your love.

He rails against the laws that conflict with the medical choices he and his wife made. He writes, "While we support laws protecting vulnerable people against involuntary sterilization, the law appears to be too broadly based to distinguish between people who are . . . capable of decision making and those who . . . [like] Ashley . . . will never become remotely capable of decision making."[5]

Listen. Not so long ago in the name of the health and strength of the nation, eugenicists would have labeled Ashley an idiot, locked her up, and sterilized her, regardless of what you wanted. Between 1899 and 1982 thirty-three states passed eugenic sterilization laws and performed more than sixty thousand involuntary hysterectomies, tubal ligations, castrations, and vasectomies. Mere decades later, who is worthy of protection? Love does not erase history.

....

A father profoundly reshapes his disabled daughter's body-mind, using surgery and hormones, and calls it love. He names her a "pillow angel" and calls it love. He protects his privacy but not hers and calls it love. He denies that she's capable of womanhood and calls it love. Fury overtakes me.

Love? You dare to call this, love? I refuse to engage on your terms.

....

I sit with a photo of Ashley taken in 2015, years after her mastectomy, hysterectomy, and high-dose estrogen treatment.[6] She's almost eighteen, sitting outside near a rhododendron bush in full bloom. The pillow she's propped against matches the bright pink blossoms. She stares beyond the camera, her face grown wider and fuller in the nine years since that Christmas photo in 2006.

I feel sorrow and rage. I think about the bioethical controversy that swirls around her. I try to come to terms with the medical procedures she underwent. I rehash her father's words.

But underneath all that is a girl lying outside in the garden, a girl dressed in pink and lavender, a girl on the cusp between adolescence and womanhood, a girl poised to join a legion of short-statured women, flat-chested women, intellectually and physically disabled women, sterilized-without-their-consent women.

I yearn for her.

Resisting Intelligence

Intelligence is used repeatedly to determine worthiness, value, and personhood. Imagine a world where *idiot, moron, retarded, slow, stupid* weren't insults and justifications for eradication, where being deemed a vegetable didn't almost always lead to the denial of the most basic human rights. IQ tests wouldn't exist. Intellectually disabled people wouldn't face the bullying, patronizing, substandard education, violence, institutionalization, exclusion, and imprisonment that they encounter today. Supposed stupidity wouldn't be used as a tool to further marginalize Black people, Indigenous peoples, immigrants, and poor people. Black and Latinx youth wouldn't be tracked from special ed to prison. Actually, special ed wouldn't exist. In its place, we'd commit to education that truly meets many different ways of learning. Terri Schiavo wouldn't be dead, and Ashley wouldn't have been subjected to a hysterectomy, mastectomy, and high doses of estrogen when she was six years old.[7]

But in today's world, being seen as intellectually, cognitively, or developmentally disabled is dangerous because intelligence and verbal communication are entrenched markers of personhood. Some of us live with this danger on a daily basis because we're actually dealing with the visceral experiences of thinking, processing information, and communicating differently than what's considered normal. Others of us are targeted because of ableist stereotypes that characterize all deaf, chronically ill, and disabled people as intellectually inferior. And still others of us who are nondisabled face this danger because of the ways racism, sexism, classism, homophobia, and xenophobia cast marginalized peoples as "defective" and "stupid." Regardless of how our brains function, the pairing of personhood with intelligence needs to change. Yet when faced with allegations or assumptions of stupidity or diminished mental capacity, many of us respond by asserting our intelligence and distancing ourselves from intellectual disability.

I think about the ways I defend myself when the bullies call *retard* and grocery store clerks, doctors, teachers, or strangers on the street talk to me loudly and slowly as if I can't understand. My most immediate response is to declare myself smart, not intellectually disabled; over and over again I've railed against the misperception of my intelligence. From the moment I started first grade, I took as much distance as I could from the kids in special ed. I tried to make it absolutely clear that I was not like them. In short, I've repeatedly used intelligence as the marker of my worth and personhood.

And I am not the only one. I think of the documentary *Wretches and Jabberers* about white, autistic men Tracy Thresher and Larry Bissonnette on a road trip around the world to meet other autistic people and debunk ableist stereotypes.[8] Neither of them had a means of communication until they were adults. They were both assumed to be intellectually disabled, Larry institutionalized at the state-run Brandon Training

School in Vermont and Tracy warehoused in special ed. Tracy recounts, "When I was twenty-three years old, I started typing. Slowly I showed my true intelligence." Of his work as an activist now, he types, "The purpose in my life is to show that people like me are intelligent." Throughout the film, both men emphasize all the ways in which they're smart. Larry types, "We're traveling the world to move people's knowledge of disability to a positive place, seeing the intelligence rather than the inability." I know well the frustration, the feeling of insult, how dangerous it is to be seen as "retarded." Yet I want to sit with these men, disabled person to disabled person, and ask, "What would happen if we weren't smart? How would we defend our lives, our worthiness, our personhood then?"[9]

Let me remind all of us—disabled and nondisabled—that every time we defend our intelligence, we come close to disowning intellectually disabled people. We imply that it might be okay to exclude, devalue, and institutionalize people who actually live with body-mind conditions that impact the ways they think, understand, and process information.

The only way out of this trap is to move toward, not away from, intellectually disabled people, to practice active solidarity. We need to challenge friends and coworkers who casually or intentionally use the word *retarded*. Support activist organizations run by developmentally and intellectually disabled people.[10] Create access. If we're teachers or researchers, take seriously the disability rights slogan, "Nothing about us without us," and apply it to our work with all disabled students and research subjects. One of the autistic people Tracy Thresher and Larry Bissonnette met in their travels types it simply: "Take us for real people. Don't sideline us."

If we resist using intelligence as a measure of worth and personhood, then it can never again be used as a weapon.

Feeling Broken

....

Cure promises wholeness even as the world pokes and prods, reverberating beneath our skin, a broken world giving rise to broken selves.

All my life, I've rebelled against the endless assumptions that my body-mind is broken. I've resisted. I've ranted. I've turned my back on brokenness. Occasionally I've tried redefining wholeness to include that which is collapsed, crushed, or shattered. But mostly I've just flat-out refused brokenness and the perceptions of weakness, vulnerability, and tragedy that come with it.

> I dream of a big pottery bowl
> painted in intricate patterns.

But however much I refuse and, in those refusals, tell an important truth, I have to say: I am also profoundly broken. My father and the cell of perpetrators to which he belonged shattered my body-mind. The violence they inflicted winds through me. I could quibble over words and call myself *damaged*. But the starker, blunter *broken* calls to me. It speaks of fragments and shards, an irrevocable fracturing. And fracture me they did, using sexual violence, physical violence, and mind control that I can only describe as torture. I won't write the details or try to capture the terror and pain in words. But believe me: what they did broke my body-mind. It shaped every part of my life. This is not hyperbole, not a claim to perpetual victimhood nor a ploy for sympathy, but rather an enraging truth.

> I turn the bowl in my hands,
> lose myself in its patterns.

Twenty years ago I walked through the world detached from body-mind and emotion, skittish, fearful of human touch, hearing voices and seeing shadows, plotting suicide. When it became clear that I had to deal with this damage or end up dead, all I wanted was to be cured.

The ideology of cure would have us believe that whole and broken are opposites and that the latter has no value.

I spent years in therapy and bodywork. I practiced self-care and built a support network. I found community. I dug into shame. I helped organize Take Back the Night marches, put together rape prevention trainings, wrote about child abuse. I never spoke directly about my desire for a cure, but really I felt desperate to fix my broken self, to emerge into a place where the twenty-four years of torture I experienced as a child and young adult simply no longer existed. I spent nearly a decade working hard at recovery—recovering lost years, memories, selves—before I knew that I'd never be cured.

> Slowly, slowly the bowl reveals itself—
> shattered and pieced back together.

My relationship to that violence is different now—my sense of self less fractured; my ability to stay in my body-mind and in the present, stronger. Yet I am nowhere near finished with its aftermath. Not long ago, paper skeletons hanging in the window of a local restaurant triggered an old memory of torture, catapulting me into a week-long dissociative fugue. Three summers ago, suicide gripped me hard, voices filling my head, seductive and terrifying. I didn't leave the house for a month.

> Those intricate patterns—a spider web
> of fractures, cracks, seams.

I'm grateful that triggers and hallucinations don't grab me in their vice grip nearly as often as they used to. Even so, I know the past will again pound through my body-mind. The voices will again scream in my head, owning me, commanding me to kill myself, self-loathing carved into my synapses. I've come to know that there will be no cure. I claim brokenness to make this irrevocable shattering visible.

> Splashes of sunlight
> filter through the cracks.

There will be no return to the moments before my father first grabbed my body-mind.

Cure dismisses resilience, survival, the spider web of fractures, cracks, and seams. Its promise holds power precisely because none of us want to be broken. But I'm curious: what might happen if we were to accept, claim, embrace our brokenness?

Being Fixed

Sometimes we can claim brokenness for ourselves, using that word to name a truth. But mostly it's claimed for us. We're broken because doctors and the media, our partners and families, coworkers and case managers say so. Amidst these voices, listening to our own body-minds is almost impossible. But even when we're able to create a bit of space to figure out what we feel, the meanings of *broken* and its companion *fixed* bend and waver.

I think of the most straightforward of breaks, imagining an accident that fractures the femur of some nondisabled walkie, making her leg unfunctional and causing her a great deal of pain. She has health insurance and a reasonably respectful primary care doctor, but since this is a crisis, she goes to the emergency room and gets her leg x-rayed. The doctor easily locates the break, sets the bone, places her leg in a cast, and sends her home. When she asks for pain meds, the doc writes her a prescription for thirty days' worth of Vicodin and, because she's a white, middle-class professional, she isn't treated like a drug-seeking criminal. Although her recovery is long and more than a bit uncomfortable as she learns to walk on under-the-arm crutches, getting a taste of how inaccessible the world is, her femur mends, bone knitting itself back together. In six months, maybe nine, her leg is so close to what it was before the accident that she no longer thinks about it. In this imagined scenario, both *broken* and *fixed* are simple and neat. If the medical-industrial complex always functioned this way, we wouldn't need to grapple with cure.

But for many disabled people, there's nothing simple or neat about broken legs and fixed legs. In disability communities, we talk about lifetimes of surgeries unchosen. For some of us, our earliest memories are of doctors bending over us, months spent sweating in plaster casts. Our body-minds display medical histories in bulky lines of scar, indentations and ridges, hypersensitivity and numbness. Doctors have stretched, straightened, twisted, untwisted, and amputated legs deemed broken.

For a lot of us physically disabled from birth or early childhood, being *fixed* means shame and pain, boredom and fear. We remember multiple hospitals, surgeons, and operating rooms. We count our surgeries in the dozens.

I escaped this disability reality. I could say I was lucky, but that luck was actually a function of geography and class. The nearest children's hospital with enough resources and orthopedic doctors to perform cerebral palsy–related surgeries was a seven-hour drive from our house in the backwoods of Oregon. So instead my parents took me to a small-town pediatrician an hour away. He was an incompetent man, one of the few doctors among whom we could choose. He never even mentioned surgery. We had health insurance, but my working-class mother and poor father believed medical care was a scarce resource to use as infrequently as possible. Neither of them had grown up with regular health care, and they had no idea how to navigate the world of doctors. They didn't know what questions to ask or demands to make. In their search for a cure for me, they rarely sought out specialists or second opinions. By turns, they were intimidated by doctors and suspicious of their expertise. During my round of diagnostic testing at the Crippled Children's Division, we did meet with an orthopedist who recommended heel cord surgery. My parents shrugged off the possibility.

This pile of rural, working-class realities shielded me from surgery, and my parents from the pressure of some persuasive orthopedic surgeon at some fancy children's hospital. And if they hadn't said no at the Crippled Children's Division, I wonder what my unsteady, rattling walk would be like today. What would *fixed* have meant?

I listen to disabled writer Jill Sager, who at the age of nine underwent surgery to "fix" her shorter left leg:

> My parents trusted the doctor. . . . [They] didn't know that the "apparatus" I was to wear for five months would eventually kill off all the nerves and muscles in my leg leaving my knee, foot, and toes with limited mobility. . . . They didn't realize that my sciatic nerve would be damaged or that my left foot would become one and a half times smaller than my right foot. . . . They didn't know that I would always walk with a limp and would later develop curvature of the spine. My parents didn't know this was called experimental surgery. They agreed to surgery to make both my legs the same size.[11]

Sager tells a common story. What she describes isn't the far edge of medical incompetence but a relatively typical experience for a physically disabled child whose parents have access to health care beyond the sheer basics. I have no idea whether Sager thinks of her leg as broken or whole, both or neither, but most likely the doctors involved in her surgeries thought of their work as a fix.

Broken legs do get *fixed* with regularity, but inside the medical-industrial complex, legs also become more *broken*—those supposed opposites wavering, bending, twining together.

Shame and Pride

Shame is a chasm of loathing lodged in our body-minds, a seemingly impenetrable fog, an unspeakable and unspoken fist. It has often become our home.

In response, folks from a variety of marginalized communities—people of color, queer and trans people, Deaf people, disabled people, fat people—have claimed self-love as an act of resistance. We've rejected the idea that our body-minds are broken. We've learned lessons from the Black Power movement of the 1960s and the slogan "Black Is Beautiful." We've rallied around the value of pride.

But make no mistake—shame isn't only the province of folks who live with oppression, isolation, and violence. I've witnessed white people, rich people, slender women, cisgender heterosexual men struggle inside that chasm of self-loathing. In one way or another, most of us have experience with shame.

It wakes us up in the morning and puts us to bed at night. It whispers to us as we have sex and sits with us as we fill out job applications. It makes snarky comments as we pull on our clothes to go out and stands next to us as we wait in line for food stamps. It visits us in medical exam rooms and at the beach. It lives in the mirror and the camera. It causes low self-esteem and drug addiction. It leads far too many of us to suicide.

And now, I need to turn directly to you, my readers, because I know shame is a matter of survival and well-being, deeply personal and overtly political. I want to invite you to dig through this raw, overwhelming mess with me. But it's hard to know where to begin because built into the sheer body-mind experience of shame is an isolation that evades language.

It's not enough to just lay out a trajectory toward pride, pausing only briefly to acknowledge the power and lasting consequences of self-hatred. Not enough to assume that people will arrive at self-acceptance through activism and shared experience. Not enough to understand the ways in which violence and prurient curiosity, the ideology of cure and media images weave together to become shame's fertile ground.

No, I want us to take a riskier course. I want us to lean directly into that seemingly impenetrable fog, that unspeakable and unspoken fist.

....

As a queer, disabled writer, I've told more than a few stories about shame, but in my telling, I've often portrayed that feeling as if it were a thing of the past, through which I had already moved. But that is a half lie. So let me tell another story—a story about shame roaring into the present. Not long ago my sweetie, Samuel, and I went on a week-long, three-hundred-mile cycling trip in the Pacific Northwest, part of a ninety-five-person tour. This story starts on the fifth day of that trip.

It is Thursday, and we head out early through drifting fog. Mount Adams, which last night towered over our campsite, has vanished into the clouds. We pedal into the first climb of the day, twenty miles up and up and up to brush by the mountain before descending back into the Colombia River Gorge. Slow and steady, I throw myself into the rhythm of my low-slung recumbent trike. Samuel and I ride side by side. I know he's hurting—neck, wrists, crotch, and feet sore in the way only an up-right bicycle can make a human body-mind sore. In contrast, my trike is a lawn chair with pedals and wheels. I remind him of his strong, sexy legs and heart, how they'll power him through today's miles.

We're ascending a paved logging road, scrubby, overgrown clearcuts alternating with the deep green of fir and spruce, remnants of old-growth forest. No cars pass us, except our own support vehicles. Twenty years ago logging trucks reigned here, but now the woods are logged out. Bikes stream by me because on my trike I am slow, slow, slow, but I've warmed up, legs pushing and pulling. I breathe the trees, the mist, the sheer motion into me. This is home.

I grew up in the backwoods, riding roads exactly like this one. On my Schwinn ten-speed, I'd race downhill, wind billowing under my T-shirt.

I'd ride the fog line or weave between the raised reflective bumps that formed the centerline. I'd sweat uphill every morning on the way to my summer job. I'd wave to each logging truck that passed by, hopeful to hear two short blasts of its air horn in return. I was in love with and inseparable from my bike. But when I moved to the city at age seventeen, I left it and my love affair behind. My balance on a two-wheeler was adequate but not good, and I knew I couldn't ride safely on city streets.

I can see Samuel in my rearview mirror, twenty-five yards behind me, the bit of swing in his shoulders telling me that his legs are finally loosened up. But what I don't know is that as people pass him by, for he is as slow as I am this morning, they're peppering him with questions: "What's wrong with Eli?" "What's his neurological condition?" "Does he have multiple sclerosis or Parkinson's?" "He's so brave; what kind of trike does he ride?" All week we've been dealing with this crap, folks assuming he's my caretaker, chaperone, guide, talking to him but not me. When they do talk to me, it's to say, "You're so amazing; I don't know how you do it," as if we're not all tapping into reserves, pushing hard in the ways that endurance adventures always demand. Samuel and I have agreed that his response to their questions needs to be "Ask Eli." But I don't know that these people are playing twenty questions with my lover because this morning no one is acting on his suggestion; no one is talking to me.

When I bought my trike three years ago, I hadn't ridden for a long time. I knew I'd enjoy pedaling the back roads again, ready for whatever adventures this new machine brought me. But I didn't expect to pick up my love affair right where I had left it.

Samuel catches up to me, we ride side by side again, and he tells me about the stream of questions. He's pissed, exhausted, anxious, and I in turn am incandescent with rage. I want to throw rocks and spit curses, not so much for myself but for the distress I see in his face. My rage, however, is short-lived. All too soon shame takes hold, and I am asking Samuel, "Do I bring you anything but grief and trouble?"

We try to process it, fifteen hundred feet of elevation into this climb, another five hundred to go. But soon I'm howling to the mountain, the trees, sobbing into the fog, "What's wrong with me, why won't they talk to me? What's wrong with me? Wrong with me. Wrong." This too is home—this isolation, desolation, inconsolable sense of wrongness.

I know that shame has become home for many of us. I am not the only one. Somehow this knowledge reassures me, even as it breaks my heart.

When I signed up for the trip, I anticipated joy, exhaustion, challenge. I trained hard, rode long miles, and knew there'd be sweat, pain, and exhilaration waiting for me. But I didn't expect this bone-deep shame. It caught me by surprise, reminding me that body-mind hatred and acceptance are not separate and opposing forces. Instead they wrestle, spar, sit at the same table. Once taught inconsolable wrongness, how do we unlearn it, return to that time before the lessons began? Or is there no return, no restoration, no cure, but rather acceptance, resistance, building anew amidst this dense thicket?

We are experts at hiding our shame, swallowing it, pretending it's not there. But to build anew, we can't be silent. I want us to paint, write, dance, roll, sing, stutter, sign, cry, laugh, kickbox our shame out. Want us to organize rallies; chalk the sidewalks; talk to our friends, lovers, partners, families. Want us to remind each other of our beauty, strength, resilience; then tape those reminders to our bathroom mirrors. Want us to read them out loud every day, even when we don't believe them.

Since returning from that trip, shame has stalked me. I ride my trike, and on every pedal stroke, I hear the long-ago bullies, echoing back, "Defect, monkey, retard." In the mirror, I see "ugly, stupid, wrong." I say to shame, "Get out. You are no longer welcome here." Sometimes I believe myself, other times not. I enlist my friends, my communities, my politics, my rage. I use other people's anger to bolster my own. I pound words onto paper. Slowly, one by one, I unpack the lies that feed my shame. I can't say I'm done; I doubt there is one definitive end to this struggle, a single transit from shame to pride.

Yet I know that the work of making our body-minds home is well worth it. There are many tunnels through the thicket, and on the other side lives an openness that lets us slide into ourselves and makes space for joy and comfort. Body-mind acceptance can wake us up in the morning, put us to bed at night, visit us as we're dressing to go out or singing along to our favorite song. These moments don't usually arrive as big and brash as a Pride parade. Rather they appear unexpectedly as we're rabble-rousing in the streets, tromping through the woods, or dancing up a storm on Friday night.

These moments allow us to turn away from *normal*. They interrupt the many ways shame hooks us into cure. They create space for our body-minds as they are right now. They foster a matter-of-fact acceptance of our tics, tremors, stutters, seizures, knots, scars, pain, quirks. They encourage an appreciation for missing teeth and the smarts that stretch food stamps to the end of the month, for big bellies and wide hips, for the flash of hands signing American Sign Language and typing on assistive communication devices, for dark skin and kinky hair. They let us embrace our wild femmeness, our handsome butchness, our glorious androgyny. I want to live in a world where these moments are common and unremarkable.

brilliant imperfection

SURVIVAL NOTES

When the voices start roaring in my head, flashbacks
thundering, self splitting from self, let me remember to eat
miso spread thick on whole-wheat toast. Sit with my dog on
the kitchen floor at three in the morning. Pour vodka down
the drain. Listen to my feet, literally listen to heels tapping
concrete, crunching gravel.

Remember to make deals with friends: agree not to
wander, not to horde alcohol and muscle relaxants, not to
leave the yard without my dog. Agree to stay alive.

Remember to weed the garden. Dig baby potatoes up by
the handful, pull baby beets out of the ground, sauté them
for breakfast. Sleep when I can and drag myself to work. Call
upon the spirits who have protected me for years. Talk to
the trees; listen to the stones. Ride the voices out until they
no longer grip me.

And when my head clears, I will return to walks in
the woods, night skies thick with stars, rhubarb pie with
friends. I promise.

10 PROMISE OF CURE

Normal and Natural

The medical-industrial complex pushes normal weight, normal walking, normal ways of thinking, feeling, and communicating as if *normal* were a goal to achieve and maintain. Sometimes *normal* is attached to *natural*; multinational corporations marketing natural beauty, natural strength, natural skin every day, as if *natural* were a product to sell.

At the same time, white Western beliefs separate human animals from nonhuman nature and devalue the natural world. Coupled with capitalism, these beliefs drive an out-of-control greed for and consumption of coal and trees, fish and crude oil, water and land. Drive the destruction of what is natural. Drive the declaration of cornfields as more productive and necessary than prairie. In short, the white Western world both desires to be *natural* and destroys what is *natural*, depending on the context. It makes no sense.

The standards called *normal*—sometimes in tandem with *natural*—are promoted as averages. They are posed as the most common and best states of being for body-minds. They are advertised as descriptions of who "we" collectively are—a *we* who predictably is white, male, middle- and upper-class, nondisabled, Christian, heterosexual, gender-conforming, slender, cisgender. And at the very same time, these standards, which supposedly reflect some sort of collective humanity, are sold back to us as goals and products. It makes no sense.

This nonsense couldn't exist without the threat of *unnatural* and *abnormal*. Whether focused on repairing disabled body-minds or straightening kinky hair, lightening brown skin or making gay, lesbian, and bi people heterosexual, cure aims to make us as *normal* and *natural* as possible. The pressure is intense, created and sustained by the consequences and dangers of being considered abnormal and unnatural. Inside this pressure cooker, the promise of cure is continually at work.

Finding Wholeness

In the years leading up to my chest reconstruction surgery, doubt gripped me. I didn't hate my breasts but still wished them gone. I sat with questions and misgivings. Only a decade and a half before, I had wanted to amputate my shaky right arm, to be done with the tremors I couldn't hide, the tension locked into shoulder and forearm. I asked myself flat out: What's the difference between these two desires—the one to amputate my breasts and the other to cut off my right arm?

I could say I never wanted breasts, drawing a straight line between the nine-year-old protesting my mother's command to put a T-shirt on and the thirty-five-year-old saving money for surgery. I could, but I would be simplifying a looping and contradictory history. No single story holds the entire truth.

I knew what body-mind hatred felt like—its desperate numbness tearing at me, willing away my lopsided flesh, clumsy gait, ugly tremors. I had worked hard to disentangle myself from the bleakest of that hatred and in the process abandoned my fantasy of cutting off an arm. But as my longing for a flat chest emerged, I returned to that work, tunneling some more through the thicket called shame. I came to trust that my gendered and sexed desire shared almost nothing in common with my disability hatred. That desire arose, quiet and insistent, not from self-loathing but rather self-love, flesh whispering, "*This,* this body-mind, is what I want." Shame and love fluttered like shadow and light.

I used this insight to explain my body-mind, first to myself, then to family, friends, and acquaintances. I leveraged shame as wrong and imposed from the outside and self-love as unassailable and entirely internal. The contrast between shame and self-acceptance became the way I justified my desire, as if what my body-mind wanted couldn't quite be trusted.

I am the genderqueer who binds my breasts tight against my chest wall, flattening them as much as possible. It is uncomfortable and necessary, another way to both ignore and love my body-mind. I start buying crisp Oxford shirts and thin retro ties, dress clothes no longer a misery.

I felt buffeted by the endless prurient questions: "How do you know you're transgender?" "Isn't surgery mutilation?" "Are you a boy or a girl?" I used my insight to shield myself. But in doing so, I was defending, rather than claiming, the yearning that streamed through me.

I am the lover who finds a way to unbind my breasts. My nipples come alive to fingers, tongue, teeth, stone melting away.

....

I could end this story right here; let my insight about shame and self-love be the resolution, the answer to my presurgery ambivalence. But I actually want something less neat, less resolved, because even today as I run my hand over my pecs, adore how my shirts fit, and feel immense comfort inside my skin, I hear echoes of my earlier self-doubt. How can I reconcile my lifelong struggle to love my disabled self exactly as it is with my use of medical technology to reshape my gendered and sexed body-mind? I'm searching for a messier story.

I return to transabled people, those folks who actively choose disability for themselves and in the process encounter so much revulsion, anger, disbelief. I have to say that I don't fully grasp their desire, but I do know that it is real and unrelenting. I could be one of those people who ask endless questions, allowing prurient curiosity to take the place of courtesy, respect, connection. Or I could quiet myself and sit with what I don't understand.[1]

In the documentary *Whole*, which profiles five white, transabled men, George recounts, "I carried out . . . a lifelong obsession that my leg should be amputated. I very methodically planned an injury with the shotgun. . . . And [after it happened], I felt absolutely . . . transformed. . . . I have become whole."[2] I sit with his words, recognizing his desperation and contentment but still not understanding transabled desire. His story makes me uneasy. Kevin, another of the men profiled in the film, says of his longing that led him to find a surgeon willing to amputate one of his legs: "I think it's weird. What is it that visits this on people? . . . It's obviously peculiar. But knowing it's peculiar . . . doesn't do away with [it]." I think about our body-mind desires and which ones we choose to follow, to trust even when they are contradictory, mystifying, inexplicable. I listen to Kevin's puzzlement, George's certainty; both feel familiar to me. Toward the end of the documentary, George reflects, "What I did that day [I shot my leg] was imperative. The alternative was suicide." I've heard the exact same sentiment in trans communities about gender transition. George's and Kevin's words, coupled with the ways I both recognize and feel unsettled by them, stir up the messiness I need.

....

I am the female-to-male transgender person who lets a scalpel touch my chest. The surgeon slices half-moons around my aureoles, cuts tissue away, and preserves as many nerves as possible. I lie in this operating room, anesthetized and in relationship with medical technology yet again.

Nothing I tried satisfied my desire for a flat chest—not denying it, not talking about it, not working to love myself more, not binding. So I went looking for a surgeon and started saving $8,000, slowly, paycheck by paycheck.

Three days later, I remove the bandages for the first time and stand in front of the mirror. I haven't seen this flat, smooth chest in a long time. Still later, after the surgeon removes my bulb drains, I button up my flannel shirt, and it fits exactly right.

I could have turned my desire into a diagnosis, named it gender identity disorder, declaring myself a man who needed a man's body-mind, and surgery a cure. But my yearning was more paradoxical than that, as is the body-mind rightness I feel now, never missing for one instant the weight, size, shape, or sensation of my breasts.

It's midsummer, and I am the white guy walking a dirt road between cornfields in occupied Dakota Territory right after sunset. I take off my T-shirt, tucking it into the waistband of my shorts. The fields are lushly green, quivering in the humidity. The cornstalks stand tall and sturdy, tassels silky and the color of honey, kernels of corn plump and hidden. Dusk licks my ribs, sternum, collarbone. I think about how good these ears of sweet corn taste, fresh from the field, husked, boiled, and buttered.

I struggle with the concept of body-mind rightness. I don't quite believe in it, even as I've felt it spread across my chest. As an idea, it suggests that we can disentangle our body-minds from all the forces the world exerts on us and feel some kind of pure, individual rightness humming under our skin. I don't believe we can separate ourselves that definitively from oppression and privilege, stereotypes and shame. And yet in my technologically reshaped flesh, I feel an abiding contentment, which I can only describe as rightness. I so need that messier story that allows our body-minds and desires to be inexplicable.

But as I walk farther down this dirt road, I remember how easy it is to mistake beauty. The monoculture of agribusiness corn has brought nothing but soil depletion and erosion, a glut of non-nutritious, corn-based processed food, and wholesale destruction of prairies. I think of the ecosystem my friends are restoring. I think yet again about natural *and* unnatural, normal *and* abnormal. *But mostly I feel dusk licking my bare skin—a soft, airy caress. It would be all too easy to mistake this individual body-mind pleasure and comfort for collective liberation.*

....

This welter of feelings and beliefs brings me back to transabled people. I still don't understand their unequivocal choice of disability. But then, I am also the person who doesn't fully understand my own visceral desires. I need that messier story because there is no real way to reconcile my lifelong struggle to love my disabled self exactly as it is with my use of medical technology to reshape my gendered and sexed body-mind. I can either try to fix the contradictions or embrace them.

In the end, I, like transabled people lucky enough to find surgeons willing to operate on them or desperate enough to carry out disabling events, had healthy flesh cut away and in the process found wholeness. Shame and love still flutter like shadow and light.

Gender Transition

My slow turn from butch dyke to genderqueer living as a white man in the world was never about curing disorder or fixing brokenness, but rather about desire and comfort—transition a door, a window, a cobalt sky.

That said, trans people who want to transition using surgeries, hormone replacement therapy, or both have many different relationships to cure. Some folks name their transness a birth defect, a disability in need of repair. The word *defect* always takes my breath away. It's a punch in my stomach. These folks reason, "I should have easy access to competent, respectful health care just as other disabled people do. I simply need a cure." Their logic makes me incredulous, even as I work to respect people who name their transness this way. Do they really believe disability ensures decent—much less good—health care? I could tell a thousand stories, cite pages of statistics, confirming the opposite, and rant for hours about ableism in the medical-industrial complex. I hate their unquestioned acceptance of cure.

But I need to pause my rant for a moment. Until the early 1990s, when trans communities began finding strong, collective voices, medical providers' explicit goal for gender transition was to create normal heterosexual men and women who never again identified as trans, gendernonconforming, gay, lesbian, or bi. In other words, the framing of transness as defect, an abnormality to be corrected, didn't start with trans people but with the medical-industrial complex.

And then there are the real forces of gender dissonance and body-mind dysphoria. Scholar Alexandre Baril reflects, "The problem with framing transness as a defect resides, I believe, not in the concept of transness as disability, but in such individualist, ableist, pathologising views of disabilities."[3] He continues, describing his experience as a transsexual disabled man: "My transness has been and continues to be a debilitating and disabling component of my life. My dysphoria, although much less intense than before my transition, is a constant presence that manifests itself through a variety of concerns that, taken separately, might seem insignificant but that, taken together, reveal a persistent discomfort about my body. This dysphoria is as psychologically disabling as my other mental disabilities."[4] Rather than resorting to some naive and stereotyped notion of defect, Baril is grappling with a complex tangle. His words ask me to sit with the reality of body-mind dysphoria as a sometimes overwhelming or disabling force.

Still other trans people turn the idea of gender dissonance inside out, refusing to name transness a disease and gender nonconformity a pathology. Their refusal locates dysphoria not in individual trans people but rather in a world that often denies, mocks, and criminalizes our genders.

Transition as an open door, transness as defect to fix, gender dysphoria as disability, transgender identities as nonpathologized body-mind difference—all these various realities exist at the same time, each with its own relationship to cure and the medical-industrial complex.

....

Even as my transition was not about fixing disorder, the promise of cure still called out to me, burrowing into my body-mind and channeling what I wanted. The medical-industrial complex taps into our desires, promising us so much. Through cure, it assures us that we can control and reshape our body-minds; restore them to some longed-for, imagined, or former state of being. Assures us that the unhappiness we feel resides within our individual selves. Assures us that on an individual level we can be whole and that on a collective level disability, illness, and body-mind difference can be eradicated. This assurance—that medical technology can align our body-minds with what we desire (whether it be an end to pain or depression, the ability to walk again, the loss of weight, or the reshaping of our sexed and gendered selves)—is so seductive.

When I started taking testosterone, I was impatient for facial hair and a deeper voice, slimmer hips and a squarer jaw. But underneath those defined body-mind changes, I hungered for a settledness that *girl* and *woman* had never given me. I caught myself thinking of that pale yellow synthetic hormone as honey and light, the smell of sugar pine, infusing me. Through metaphor, I was trying to wrench my transformation away from the medical-industrial complex.

But in truth, the people who control transition technology—surgeons, therapists, endocrinologists, family doctors—are all embedded in the white Western system of medicine, trained to identify and repair body-mind trouble. Diagnosis in the form of gender dysphoria and the recently discarded gender identity disorder plays a significant role in who receives treatment in the form of hormones and surgery and who doesn't. Multinational pharmaceutical companies develop, produce, distribute, and profit from hormones. In short, the medical-industrial complex shapes gender transition in dozens of ways. I wasn't injecting honey and light into me but rather a chemical compound, contributing to the profits of Sun Pharmaceutical Industries. I was stepping through the door held open by the promise of cure.

....

Trans people aren't alone in our encounters with the promise of cure. Any time we—trans and cisgender, disabled and nondisabled—access medical technology to change our body-minds in little ways or big ways, we are engaging with that seductive assurance. We go to a fertility clinic wanting to become pregnant, to our primary care doctor wanting meds to stop daily full-blown panic attacks, to the emergency room wanting to mend a broken leg. We enter the medical-industrial complex with many different needs and desires, interacting with cure's promise in many different ways.

But cure doesn't only follow the lead of our body-mind yearnings; it also pushes us toward normality. Transition certainly didn't make me a normal guy. Yet I'm no longer "ma'am" on one street corner and "sir" on the next—my body-mind no longer a pry bar, leveraging space between man and woman. For the first time in my life, I'm read consistently as a single gender. Even as I've remained twisted, bent, rebellious, unrepentantly queer, my relationship to *normal* has definitely changed.

....

The promise of cure held the door open, and I stepped through. I listened to desire. I found body-mind comfort. I live more easily inside the gender binary. I still feel akin to my nine-year-old self who flew her kite in the hayfields and knew she was neither girl nor boy. I cured nothing because there was nothing to cure. All these forces jostle through me.

Bullied

....

Annette, you and I met thirty years ago walking across the United States on the Great Peace March for Global Nuclear Disarmament.[5] We shared a tent for those eight and a half months and still call each other tentmates. Such an intimate relationship—neither sisters nor lovers—we slept together in a rose-colored dome tent night after night across the desert, mountains, Great Plains, through cornfields, cities, and industrial sprawl. A decade and a half later, we fell apart over body-mind change.

The same year I had chest reconstruction surgery, you had gastric bypass surgery. Neither of us liked the choice the other was making. You wanted me to stay a woman, and I wanted you to remain fat. As someone who loves your breasts, you had no understanding of why I wanted mine gone. And I, with a long history of appreciating fat women, had no understanding of how fatness itself, not only fatphobia and shame about being fat, was trouble in your life. Your feminist politics made gender transition hard to accept, and my fat politics made weight loss surgery equally unpalatable. We ended up explaining and justifying our body-minds to each other.

Annette, I remember an evening camped on Powerline Road, middle of the Mojave Desert. The whole ungainly lot of us—feminists and anarchists, middle-of-the-road Democrats and socialist revolutionaries, longtime peace activists and Vietnam vets—erupted in anger as we tried to work through some contentious community issue. That evening, you slipped me a love note on a scrap of paper. Last year I reread my journal from those months and found your note tucked inside.

I don't want to repeat the hurtful things we said to each other as we fought about surgery. In all my years of doing ally work in fat activist communities, I had never been close to anyone who decided to undergo gastric bypass. And in your time in queer communities, you had never seen anyone through gender transition. I wanted you to work against fatphobia and love your fat body-mind, just as you wanted me to fight sexism, homophobia, the gender binary and love my butch woman's body-mind. I didn't trust doctors to reshape your gastrointestinal tract and wondered if you were under the thrall of a highly profitable, well-advertised bariatric surgery industry and a media-driven panic about the "obesity epidemic."[6] Likewise, you suspected I had caved to masculinity and misogyny. We both responded with a singular, determined "change the world, not our body-minds" politics, distrusting each other's desires. In short, we were a hot mess.

Annette, I remember an afternoon at the Rocky Flats nuclear weapons plant as hundreds of us sat in front of the main gate, mountains to our backs, protesting weapons, war, radiation leaks. You and I sat close, leaning against each other.

We came back together through love, patience, time, and listening, you a smaller, but still fat, white dyke and me a genderqueer who lives as a white guy in the world. We both talked about how audacious our decisions felt, allowing scalpels and synthetic hormones to rearrange fundamental body-mind functions. We witnessed each other's changes. You shed pounds as my voice deepened; your eating shifted as I grew stubble on my face.

Listening and patience helped us through this deep struggle, but we both needed to do other work as well. You had to grow beyond your sense of transition as abandonment and betrayal into a wider understanding of gender that the binary denies. I had to embrace contradiction, letting your choices and my politics jostle against each other rather than insisting on some simple resolution. For me, compassion had to become as important as struggle. In the end, we were both transformed and utterly the same.

Annette, I remember a night camped at a racetrack on Lake Erie, our tent flapping wildly in the wind. We fell asleep giddy and laughing.

....

On the phone you tell me, "I was desperate not to be fat." We talk for a long time about desperation. You wonder out loud if your surgery was a cop-out. I ask about fatphobia—the daily jokes, laughter, whispers behind your back, outright street harassment. I remember your stories: doctors calling you "morbidly obese" and strangers heckling you on airplanes. I feel your exhaustion in my bones. I think about the gender binary and the unending trouble I've encountered in public restrooms; the daily routine of "ma'am, oh, sorry, sir, I mean ma'am" at coffee shops, gas stations, grocery stores; the frat boys who shout at me from their cars—how it all has worn me down.

Together we name fatphobia, transphobia, and the gender binary bullies, our body-mind politics still fierce but more flexible. Both of us spent our childhoods tormented, you called *fatso* and *Mama Mammoth*, me *retard* and *monkey*. I want to go back in time to sit with the twelve-year-old you who turned all that taunting inward, hating yourself more every day. Sit with you twenty-five years later as you decided to have surgery, desperate and full of desire. Sit with you now.

As children, we resisted, hid, ran away, changed ourselves, taunted right back, but none of these strategies stopped the bullies or the damage they inflicted. We swallowed the hurt, caved to their demands, cried our eyes out, fell silent. Now, as adults, we live in fat community, disability community, queer and trans community. We've found lovers and friends, demonstrated in the streets, and led anti-oppression trainings. Even so, we sometimes still swallow the hurt.

So many external forces pushed and pulled at us as you chose surgery and I chose transition. Certainly exhaustion, shame, and desperation factored into our decisions. But right now, right here, as we say good night and end our call, I can feel us holding space for each other, our stories overlapping and colliding, love humming between us.

A Maze of Contradictions

i.

Grappling with cure has led me into a maze of contradictions and colliding forces. Making profit sits next to extending life. Insisting on eradication piles on top of providing comfort. Ending pain and suffering justifies the vilest of research. All of it lives publicly in an amorphous tangle called the medical-industrial complex and privately in our bedrooms, kitchens, and bathrooms. Inside this maze, I keep stumbling into dead ends, revisiting the same intersections, discovering well-worn paths that circle back onto themselves.

I, along with many of us, am alive because of medical technology and the ideology of cure, which drives the discovery and development of that technology. Yet cure also responds to the "trouble" of being fat with gastric bypass surgery, dieting, and shaming. I have found body-mind comfort and connection through the medical-industrial complex. Yet cure also responds to the "trouble" of significant facial birthmarks with laser surgery and the "trouble" of walking in ways deemed broken by breaking bones, resetting them, stretching them. Without hesitation, I use antibiotics, ibuprofen, synthetic testosterone, appreciating everything they do for me. Yet cure also responds to the "trouble" of voices and visions with mind-numbing psychotropic medication. This maze repeats itself endlessly.

I entered it hoping to find places where all the contradictions met matter-of-factly. But now I want to step out. Step out of these constrained and constraining corners, roundabouts and dead ends. Step out and let cure be the contradictory mess it is.

ii.

Once fatphobia, ableism, sexism, racism, classism, homophobia, transphobia, xenophobia, and all the rigid constraints placed on body-mind variation are dismantled, what will we desire? This question overwhelms me. It requires an impossible flight of imagination. So let me start with what I know for sure.

No to Fairview, the Colony in Lynchburg, the Asylum in Ionia, the Judge Rotenberg Educational Center. No to the La Frontera Psychiatric Health Facility where Alexander Goodrum spent his last days and the Bronx Zoo where Ota Benga lived with Dohong the orangutan. No to ethics committees that define personhood and approve growth attenuation treatments, like the one Ashley underwent. No to generations of removal and genocide. No to daily bullying, gawking, and endless prurient questions. No to the Foundation for a Better Life selling the virtue of overcoming and the Muscular Dystrophy Association using pity and tragedy to fund-raise. No to coal-burning power plants and agribusiness cornfields, undrinkable water and unbreathable air. I sit amidst a great cloud of noes.

I catch glimpses of a world where many kinds of body-mind difference will be valued and no one eradicated; where comfort, pain, well-being, birth, and death all exist. Cure promises us so much, but it will never give us justice. In this world reconfigured, cure may not exist, but if it does, it will be only one tool among many. In this world, our body-mind desires will spread through us, as vibrant and varied as a tallgrass prairie in midsummer.

Mama, What Will You Swear?

My mother is a woman with one kidney, one ovary, and lungs that often forget how to breathe, made worse by thirty years of smoking; a woman who is allergic to half of everything that grows outside; a woman of unrelenting, sleep-all-day depression. She called me *handicapped*, a word I believed for a long time that she had invented to describe me.

But she never called herself that, even as she remembered long childhood nights spent gasping for one breath after another, hour upon hour. Her mother would gather her up, and they'd sit together in the living room, shadows thrown against the walls, lungs heaving, diaphragm straining.

On Battle Rock Beach, she and I hunted for glass floats—those green-blue, hollow glass balls Japanese fishermen used to buoy their fishing nets. In lulls between winter storms, we found them, glinting in the sun, after they had broken loose and been tumbled, tossed, blown across the ocean. Some of them arrived on the beach still wrapped in fishing net.

Daughter of a car mechanic, first generation to grow up in the city and finish high school, she learned early how to breathe air thicker than water. There was never enough money for an inhaler, much less visits to the emergency room during the worst of her attacks. *Mama, what would you have given on those desperate nights for a shot of adrenaline to open the collapsed sacks of your lungs?* She grew up, a girl living on the edge of oxygen and panic, never trusting her next breath.

She became the mother who never connected her body-mind differences to mine, her desire to have me cured palpable between us. She watched her mother have one stroke, then another, blindness descending, before she died alone and confused in a nursing home. My mother counted the women in her family—sister, aunt, mother, grandmother, great-grandmother—to die of blood clotting in the brain and heart. She swore against dying like that.

Today Japanese fishing nets are buoyed with plastic floats—white and orange, shaped like bowling pins—that no one collects, except commercial fishermen. I have a single glass float from our walks on those storm-lulled beaches—the size of a baseball and pockmarked, an ordinary object turned rare.

As her lungs grew worse—all those years of smoking Pall Malls in public, corncob pipes in private taking their toll—she taped a Do Not Resuscitate order (DNR) to her refrigerator and supported Oregon's physician-assisted suicide law. She swore against living with emphysema.

But the blood clot that rushed her brain heeded no one's sworn desires. It left her alive and immobile, sent language reeling into the netherworld. She spent months in rehab, learning the art of maneuvering a wheelchair with one floppy arm. Speech therapy returned some—but not enough—words to the warm cave of her mouth.

She used to make her way through the world with words, studying old Icelandic ballads, teaching Shakespeare and Milton, retelling the stories of King Arthur and Beowulf. She grew up with a single book—the King James Bible—and believed literacy and worthiness to be bound together.

Mama, what do you swear now as you gasp words, thicker than water, from your reordered brain? What do you want from your own bent body-mind with a heart that pumps blood prone to clotting, you who never wanted me as I was?

When you go to the grocery store, post office, movie theater, shuffling your wheelchair along with your feet, and encounter some coworker from a decade ago, what do you want? In that moment as he pats your head and kisses your cheek, murmurs some useless platitude and rushes away before your tongue can find even a single stumbling word, do you want to roll over his sensitive toes? Kick him in the shins? Flip him off with your stronger left hand? Or do you just want to retreat?

She used to tell me that I had to accept all the pity, charity, patronizing heaped on me, a fifteen-year-old trying to make sense of strangers who cried and prayed over me. *But now, let me tell you a secret: you can kick the bastard and then tell the story in all its infuriating and comic detail.*

If this float were ever to break, all I would have left is the body-mind memory of palm curving around ocean-drenched glass—those blue-green balls no longer shaped by glassblowers, broken loose from fishing nets, and found glistening in the surf on faraway beaches. And if memory were ever to be fractured, shards of glass sharp and unyielding, what then?

....

Come join us—a multitude of mad, sick, disabled, and deaf people. We won't ask you to check your shame and loss at the door. We are not Pollyannas or poster children, inspirations or tragedies. Rather we are cranky and stubborn, defining neither beauty nor ugliness, punishment nor reward. We won't ask you to desire your life, but among us, you might choose to tuck that DNR away.

Mama, what will you swear?

Walking in the Prairie Again

I return again in early fall to the thirty acres of restored tallgrass prairie in occupied Dakota Territory. I walk, thinking not of concepts, but of beings. The grasses swish against me. A few swallowtail butterflies still hover. A white-throated sparrow sings. I see coyote scat next to the path. I hear a rustle and imagine a white-footed mouse scurrying and a red fox pouncing. Above, vultures circle on the thermals. A red-tailed hawk cries not so far away.

In this moment, the prairie is made up of millions of beings. But just over the rise, another agribusiness cornfield turns brown and brittle.

Just over the rise is a barbed-wire fence, a two-lane dirt road, an absence of bison. Just over the rise is the illogic of *natural* and *unnatural*, *normal* and *abnormal*. Just over the rise, we wrestle with loss and desire, promise and injustice. Just over the rise are the bullies with their rocks and fists, the words *monkey*, *defect*, and *retard*. Just over the rise, we need to choose between monocultures and biodiversities, eradication and uncontainable flourishing.

This little pocket of restored prairie is not a return to the past nor a promise to the future, although it may hold glimmers of both. Rather it is simply an ecosystem in transition from cornfield to tallgrass, summer to winter. I feel the old corn furrows underfoot, the big bluestem waving above me, my own heart beating, imperfect and brilliant. I walk—a tremoring, slurring human, slightly off balance, one being among many. Could it all be this complexly woven and yet simple?

CYCLING

You and I are cycling buddies, you on your handcycle and
me on my recumbent trike. We make a good match, both of
us on three wheels, sitting ten inches off the ground. You
fly downhill, way faster than me; I adore watching you lean
into the first turn of a descent before you disappear. Maybe
I climb faster than you, but only maybe.

    We seek out hilly loops in western Massachusetts,
training for a three-day hundred-mile ride in New
Hampshire's White Mountains. We curse and groan our way
up Mount Tom, sail back down. On flats, we gab and tease.
When there's not enough room to ride side by side, I follow
close behind you, charting my course on bumpy asphalt
by watching your tires, admiring your shoulders flexing
through every pedal stroke. On steep hills, you tuck in
behind me, watch my rear wheel, and keep cranking.

    When we're in the White Mountains, climbing the
Kancamagus—fourteen hundred feet of elevation gain in
the last four miles—you'll slide behind me, and we'll ride
together, quiet except for the creak of your handcycle and

the wind whipping around us. Those four miles will take us well over an hour. There'll be no pity, no tragedy, no standing ovations, no over-the-top inspirational human-interest stories in the local paper; just the two of us moving slowly and steadily, defying gravity.

A Note on Reading This Book

1 Many thanks to Angela Carter, Joe Kadi, and Susan Burch for helping me think through trigger warnings for this book. For more about trauma, content notes, and trigger warnings, see Carter, "Teaching with Trauma"; Kafer, "Un/Safe Disclosures."

1. Ideology of Cure

1 For an image of the billboard, see Foundation for a Better Life, "Overcaem Dyslexia," Values.com, accessed July 8, 2009, http://www.values.com/inspirational-sayings-billboards/20-hard-work. See also Alison Kafer's critique of the FBL in *Feminist, Queer, Crip*, 86–102.

2 *Christopher Reeve: Hope in Motion* (dir. Matthew Reeve, 2007). All the quotes from Reeve and his doctor come from this film.

3 For an overview of ecosystem restoration, see Jordan, *The Sunflower Forest*.

2. Violence of Cure

1 For more on the impact of ableism on white women's suffrage, slavery, immigration, and LGB identities, see, for example, Nielsen, *A Disability History of the United States*; Boster, *African American Slavery and Disability*; Barclay, "Mothering the 'Useless'"; Baynton, "Disability and the

Justification of Inequality in American History"; Kafer, "Compulsory Bodies."

2 Cartwright, "Report on the Diseases and Physical Peculiarities of the Negro Race," 693.

3 Cartwright, "Report on the Diseases and Physical Peculiarities of the Negro Race," 712.

4 Bromberg and Simon, "The 'Protest' Psychosis," 155.

5 Bromberg and Simon, "The 'Protest' Psychosis," 155.

6 All the quotes by Darren Wilson come from "State of Missouri v. Darren Wilson," Grand Jury Volume V, September 16, 2014, 212–28, https:// www.washingtonpost.com/apps/g/page/national/read-darren-wilsons -full-grand-jury-testimony/1472/.

7 My analysis of Darren Wilson's testimony springboards from Bouie, "Michael Brown Wasn't a Superhuman Demon."

8 Johnson, *Too Late to Die Young*, 207–8.

9 Natoli et al., "Prenatal Diagnosis of Down Syndrome." For more about the history of abortion and disability, see Reagan, *Dangerous Pregnancies*.

10 "Conjoined Twins Separated in Florida," video, ABC News, May 12, 2015, http://abcnews.go.com/Health/conjoined-twins-separated-florida /story?id=30981266.

11 Quoted in Dreger, *One of Us*, 103.

12 For more on Schiavo and bioethical debates, see, for example, Asch, "Recognizing Death While Affirming Life"; Johnson, "Terri Schiavo and the Disability Rights Movement."

3. In Tandem with Cure

1 Ferguson et al., *"Away from the Public Gaze,"* 1.

2 Black, *War against the Weak*, 78. See also Larson, *Sex, Race, and Science*.

3 Kaelber, "Eugenics." See also Largent, "'The Greatest Curse of the Race.'"

4 Laughlin, *Eugenical Sterilization in the United States*, 33.

5 *Where's Molly: A True Story of Those Lost and Found* (dir. Jeff Daley, 2007).

6 *In Our Care* (1959), Vimeo, posted 2008, http://vimeo.com/365508.

7 My analysis is greatly influenced by Chimamanda Ngozi Adichie's thinking about single stories. See Adichie, "The Danger of a Single Story."

8 *Where's Molly: A True Story of Those Lost and Found* (dir. Jeff Daley, 2007).

9 *In Our Care* (1959), Vimeo, posted 2008, http://vimeo.com/365508.

10 My thinking about removal, institutionalization, and diagnosis has been shaped significantly by work about the impact of Canton Asylum for Insane Indians on Indigenous families, communities, and nations. See Yellow Bird, "Wild Indians." For more about removal, see Child, *Boarding*

School Seasons; Green and Perdue, *The Cherokee Nation and the Trail of Tears*; Jacobs, *A Generation Removed*.

11 All the quotes by former Fairview residents come from *Voices from Fairview* (2004), Vimeo, posted January 26, 2010, https://vimeo.com /8996996.

12 Gonnerman, "The School of Shock," 38.

13 Gonnerman, "The School of Shock," 38.

14 For more about the relationships among diagnosis, ableism, disability, and genocide, see Teuton, "Disability in Indigenous North America"; Burch, "'Dislocated Histories'"; Erevelles and Minear, "Unspeakable Offenses"; Poore, "Disability in Nazi Culture"; Mostert, "Useless Eaters."

4. Nuances of Cure

1 "Corpus Christi Yard Sign," Sierra Club advertisement, accessed May 20, 2016, http://content.sierraclub.org/creative-archive/sites/content .sierraclub.org.creative-archive/files/pdfs/100_92_CorpusChristiEPA _YardSign_01_low.pdf.

2 "Mercury Ad," Sierra Club advertisement, accessed May 20, 2016, https://content.sierraclub.org/creative-archive/sites/content.sierraclub .org.creative-archive/files/pdfs/100_22_DC_MercuryAd_21x22_10_low .pdf.

3 In asking for solidarity, the Sierra Club needs to more directly name the racialized and classed reality that most often it's poor people, working-class people, and people of color who work and live amidst environmental damage. Other ads in this campaign recognize the impacts of race and class. One reads, "Unfortunately, the reality is that pollution from coal-fired power plants disproportionately affects low-income communities and people of color" ("All Families Deserve to Be Together in a Just, Healthy and Clean Environment," Sierra Club advertisement, accessed November 8, 2015, http://content.sierraclub.org/creative-archive/sites /content.sierraclub.org.creative-archive/files/pdfs/0568-NACCP-8x11Ad _BW_04_low.pdf).

4 For more about environmental politics and disability, see Ray, *The Ecological Other*; Kafer, *Feminist, Queer, Crip*, 129–48.

5 Mairs, *Waist-High in the World*, 121–22.

6 For more about the Abenaki Nation and its ongoing survival and resistance, see Wiseman, *The Voice of the Dawn*.

7 I owe much of my thinking about the relationship between restoration and time to Alison Kafer's, Ellen Samuels's, and Ibby Grace's thinking about time, and in particular crip time.

8 Clare, *Exile and Pride*, 122–23.

9 Munson, "The Invisible Panelist."

10 Wendell, "Unhealthy Disabled," 18.

11 Alexander John "Bear" Goodrum (1960–2002) was a good acquaintance, a writer, an activist, and the founder of TGNet Arizona. He died in September 2002 at the age of forty-two.

12 I use the word *trans* as an inclusive umbrella term to name a wide range of transsexual, transgender, genderqueer, nonbinary, and gender-nonconforming people.

13 Quoted in Rudacille, *The Riddle of Gender*, 276.

5. Structure of Cure

1 For more about the medical-industrial complex, including a brilliant visual representation of it, see Mingus, "Medical Industrial Complex Visual."

2 Johnson, *Too Late to Die Young*, 1–2.

3 Stein, "From Activist to 'Passivist,'" 169.

4 Nestle, "When Tiredness Gives Way to Tiredness," 41.

5 See, for instance, Showalter, *Hystories*.

6 Cohen and Cosgrove, *Normal at Any Cost*, 279–81, 351.

7 A telling exception is the use of *affluenza*, which was leveraged in a 2013 court case to defend Ethan Couch, a rich white teenager who killed four people in a drunk-driving accident. The *Guardian* describes affluenza in this context as "indicating that [Couch's] behavioural problems were influenced by a troubled upbringing in a wealthy family where privilege prevented him from grasping the consequences of his actions" (Dart, "Texas Teenager Suffering 'Affluenza' Avoids Jail for Second Time"). This "disorder," not officially recognized by the medical-industrial complex, is being used here not to define wealth or class privilege as body-mind trouble but to protect a rich white teenage boy. Thanks to Alison Kafer for bringing affluenza to my attention and helping me think about it.

8 Cohen and Cosgrove, *Normal at Any Cost*, 65.

9 For more details about the FDA hearing, see Cohen and Cosgrove, *Normal at Any Cost*, 269–305.

10 For more about fatness, dieting, and weight loss surgery, see Rothblum and Solovay, *The Fat Studies Reader*.

11 Mire, "Skin-Bleaching," 15.

12 Hunter, "The Persistent Problem of Colorism," 248.

13 Quoted in Mire, "Skin-Bleaching," 15.

14 *Crip* in some disability communities is a reclaimed word, akin to *queer*. It shortens the hurtful *cripple* and infuses it with humor and communal pride.

6. How Cure Works

1 "In Her Dreams PSA," Muscular Dystrophy Association advertisement, accessed February 8, 2004, http://mda.org/media/psas. For a critique of fund-raising via telethons, particularly the MDA's Labor Day Telethon, see Johnson, *Too Late to Die Young*, 47–75.

2 "Can't Walk PSA," Muscular Dystrophy Association advertisement, accessed January 2, 2012, http://mda.org/media/psas.

3 For a historical study of disability and charity, see Longmore, *Telethons*.

4 Billy Mann and Alfonso Cuarón, "I Am Autism," 2009, YouTube, posted December 11, 2013, https://www.youtube.com/watch?v=8mycxSJ3-_Q.

5 Canadian Cystic Fibrosis Foundation, "Drowning on the Inside," YouTube, posted May 2, 2008, https://www.youtube.com/watch?v=YQajfUGWcIo.

6 "About Zoe's Race," Zoe's Race, accessed December 12, 2015, http://zoesrace.com/about-zoes-race.

7 Some culturally deaf people use the word *Deaf* with a capital *D* to refer to culturally deaf people—people whose sense of self and identity is closely connected to being deaf and who often participate in vibrant Deaf cultures—and the word *deaf* with a lowercase *d* to refer to all deaf and hard-of-hearing people. Culturally Deaf experiences and identities are often collective and communal, shaped by the use of sign language and a strong sense of community. See, for example, Humphries and Padden, *Inside Deaf Culture*; Ladd and Lane, "Deaf Ethnicity, Deafhood, and Their Relationship." Other culturally deaf people use the phrase *culturally deaf* rather than *Deaf*. I've chosen to use the word *Deaf*.

8 "My Child Was Born Deaf," Cochlear, accessed February 4, 2014, http://www.cochlear.com/wps/wcm/connect/au/home/understand/my-child-was-born-deaf.

9 Mitchiner and Sass-Lehrer, "My Child Can Have More Choices," 72.

10 Paludneviciene and Harris, "Impact of Cochlear Implants on the Deaf Community," 6.

11 For more about Deaf-gain, see Bauman and Murray, *Deaf Gain*.

12 Mitchiner and Sass-Lehrer, "My Child Can Have More Choices," 73.

13 Quoted in Mitchiner and Sass-Lehrer, "My Child Can Have More Choices," 89.

14 As a side note, this naming also connects cure back to Christianity and the long biblical tradition that casts the curing of illness and disability as miracle.

15 For more on profit making and the medical-industrial complex, see Shah, *The Body Hunters*.

16 Bristol-Myers Squibb Company, "Beauty About-Face," six-page supplement, *Cosmopolitan*, January 2001.

Brilliant Imperfection: Rolling

1 *Walkie* is a disability community word used to describe someone who walks rather than rolls. The intention behind this word isn't to create a rigid walking/rolling binary but rather to name a mode of mobility that is taken for granted and privileged in this ableist world.

7. At the Center of Cure

1 A. H. Estabrook, "Carrie and Emma Buck at the Virginia Colony for Epileptics and Feebleminded," photograph, 1924 (University of Albany, SUNY, Estabrook, SPE,XMS 80.9, box 1, folder 1-41), Eugenics Archive, no. 1287, accessed April 1, 2016, http://www.eugenicsarchive.org /eugenics/view_image.pl?id=1287.

2 Whenever possible, I've anchored my imagination of Carrie's voice in what's known of the Buck family, including Carrie; her mother, Emma; her daughter, Vivian; her sister, Doris; her brother, Roy; and her first husband, William Eagle. Of particular importance in my writing was Wendy Blair's NPR interview with Carrie, Doris, and Doris's husband Matthew Figgins from 1981 (Blair, "To Raise the Intelligence of the State"). To fill in the many holes in the record, I've both added fiction-alized details based on actual events and imagined wholesale the shape of Carrie's daily life. All of the other material in this piece reflects what is known about eugenics, sterilization, and antimiscegenation laws and practices in Virginia in the 1920s.

3 "Carrie Buck's photograph of her wedding to Mr. Eagle," photograph, 1933 (Cold Spring Harbor Laboratory Archives), Eugenics Archive, no. 2283, accessed April 1, 2016, http://www.eugenicsarchive.org/eugenics /view_image.pl?id=2283.

4 "Carrie Buck, from 'The Progress of Eugenical Sterilization,' by Paul Popenoe, *Journal of Heredity* (vol. 25:1)," photograph, 1934 (Cold Spring Harbor Laboratory Archives), Eugenics Archive, no. 2299, accessed April 1, 2016, http://www.eugenicsarchive.org/eugenics/view_image .pl?id=2299.

5 Laughlin, *Eugenical Sterilization in the United States.*

6 Quoted in Lombardo, *Three Generations, No Imbeciles,* 5.

7 Buck v. Bell, 274 U.S. 200 (1927).

8 Buck v. Bell, 274 U.S. 200 (1927).

9 For more on Central State Hospital and the history of African Americans and mental health systems, see Jackson, "In Our Own Voice"; Jackson, "Separate and Unequal."

10 Quoted in Black, *War against the Weak,* 169.

11 Blair, "To Raise the Intelligence of the State."

12 The conversation between Doris and Carrie is fictional but builds on the class-action lawsuit filed in 1980 by the American Civil Liberties Union on behalf of the people sterilized by the state of Virginia under the 1924 sterilization law. Doris Buck was one of the plaintiffs. For more details, see Lombardo, *Three Generations, No Imbeciles*, 251–54.

13 Quoted in Black, *War against the Weak*, 173–74.

14 Quoted in Lombardo, *Three Generations, No Imbeciles*, 250.

15 Quoted in Lombardo, *Three Generations, No Imbeciles*, 215.

16 Lombardo, *Three Generations, No Imbeciles*, 190.

17 See, for example, Ordover, *American Eugenics*; Larson, *Sex, Race, and Science*.

18 See "Emma Buck's Grave," photograph, 2009 (source: *Buck v Bell Documents*, Paper 61, http://readingroom.law.gsu.edu/buckvbell/61), accessed April 1, 2016, http://buckvbell.com/gallery.html; and for a report of Emma Buck's numbered gravestone, see Black, *War against the Weak*, 122.

19 "Last Photograph of Carrie Buck," photograph, 1982 (Cold Spring Harbor Laboratory Archives), Eugenics Archive, no. 2284, accessed April 1, 2016, http://www.eugenicsarchive.org/eugenics/view_image.pl?id=2284.

20 Franklin, "Authorized Sterilization Leads to Long Search."

21 This quote and all the following quotes by Jeff Daly are from his documentary *Where's Molly: A True Story of Those Lost and Found* (2007).

22 *Voices from Fairview* (2004), Vimeo, posted January 26, 2010, https://vimeo.com/8996996.

23 Bromberg and Simon, "The 'Protest' Psychosis."

24 All the case file phrases are quoted in Metzl, *The Protest Psychosis*, 148–50.

25 Metzl, *The Protest Psychosis*, 164. Many more men than women were locked up at Ionia State Hospital, and of the women who were there, almost none were women of color.

26 Metzl, *The Protest Psychosis*, 67.

27 "Signor Farini (William Leonard Hunt) with Krao," 1883, albumen silver print, Wikimedia Commons, posted February 21, 2011, https://commons.wikimedia.org/wiki/File:Signor_Farini_%28William_Leonard_Hunt%29_with_Krao,_1883.jpg.

28 Cuvier, *The Animal Kingdom Arranged in Conformity with Its Organization*, 97.

29 Vogt, *Lectures on Man*, 195, 198.

30 Quoted in Bradford and Blume, *Ota Benga*, 255.

31 For more about Ota Benga, see Newkirk, *Spectacle*.

32 Verner, *Pioneering in Central Africa*, 276.

33 Verner, *Pioneering in Central Africa*, 276.

34 Bradford and Blume, *Ota Benga*, 181.

35 New York Zoological Society, "African Pygmy. Ota Benga and Chimpanzee," photograph, 1906, Encyclopedia Virginia, accessed April 1, 2016,

http://www.encyclopediavirginia.org/slide_player?mets_filename
=sld1207mets.xml.

36 "Polly and Dohong; Chimpanzee and Orang Utan New York Zoological Park—Front," postcard, Digital Culture of Metropolitan New York, accessed October 2, 2014, http://dcmny.org/islandora/object/bronxpark %3A2911.

37 For these photos of humans and chimpanzees, see Spiegel, *The Dreaded Comparison*, 62–63.

38 For more about the Tuskegee Syphilis Study, see Reverby, *Examining Tuskegee*; Reverby, *Tuskegee's Truths*. For more about Willowbrook, see Rothman and Rothman, *The Willowbrook Wars*; Goode et al., *History and Sociology of the Willowbrook State School*. For more about the dermatology experiments at Holmesburg, see Washington, *Medical Apartheid*, 244–52; Hornblum, *Acres of Skin*.

39 Taylor, "Beasts of Burden," 194–95.

40 Haldol advertisement, *Archives of General Psychiatry* 31, no. 5 (1974): 732–33; reprinted in Metzl, *The Protest Psychosis*, fig. 1, xiv.

8. Moving through Cure

1 "Drive Stupid and Score Some Kickin' New Wheels," Don't Drive Stupid advertisement, accessed April 4, 2016, http://2.bp.blogspot.com /_iw4mpIACIU4/S3axcnaXowI/AAAAAAAAACk/BjJhuz4DSmA/s1600 -h/dontdrivestupid-001.jpg.

2 For more about transabled people, see Stevens, "Interrogating Transability"; *Whole* (dir. Melody Gilbert, 2003).

3 For more about environmental injustice and long-term processes that harm both the human and the nonhuman world, see, for example, Nixon, *Slow Violence and the Environmentalism of the Poor*.

4 "Bison Skull Pile," photograph, circa 1870 (Burton Historical Collection, Detroit Public Library), Wikimedia Commons, accessed April 4, 2016, https://commons.wikimedia.org/wiki/File:Bison_skull_pile-restored.jpg.

5 Erdoes and Lame Deer, *Lame Deer, Seeker of Visions*, 269.

6 Smits, "The Frontier Army and the Destruction of the Buffalo," 328. For more about bison and Native peoples, see Jawort, "Genocide by Other Means."

7 For more about intersex politics and the medical treatment of intersex people, see the website Intersex Initiative, accessed December 22, 2015, http://www.intersexinitiative.org; Emi Koyama, "'Zines by Intersex Initiative," Eminism.org, accessed December 22, 2015, http://eminism.org /store/zine-intersex.html.

8 For details, see WPATH, "The Standards of Care—Historical Compilation of Versions 1–6."

9 For more detail, see Lev, "Gender Dysphoria."

10 For more detail, see WPATH, "The Standards of Care—Historical Compilation of Versions 1–6."

11 Lev, "Gender Dysphoria."

12 Gloria Thomas (not her real name) was a writer and close friend when I was twenty and twenty-one. See the billboard Foundation for a Better Life, "Overcaem Dyslexia," Values.com, accessed July 8, 2009, http://www.values.com/inspirational-sayings-billboards/20-hard-work.

13 *Whoopi Goldberg: Live on Broadway* (dir. Thomas Schlamme, 1985).

14 For more about whiteness in the disability rights movement and people of color identifying as disabled, see Morales et al., "Sweet Dark Places"; Morales, *Kindling*; Schalk, "Coming to Claim Crip"; Thompson, "#DisabilityTooWhite."

15 Morales et al., "Sweet Dark Places," 94–95.

16 Hershey, "Translating the Crip."

9. Impacts of Cure

1 *Ashley's Blog*, accessed January 4, 2016, http://www.pillowangel.org.

2 "Our Interview for an In-Progress Documentary," *Ashley's Blog*, May 2015, http://www.pillowangel.org/Docu%20Interview.htm.

3 "Ashley's Family's Christmas Photo in 2006," accessed April 10, 2009, https://picasaweb.google.com/107733536573540118330/AshleyAlong TheYears?authkey=Gv1sRgCIyG7KeZo5mmCQ#5596758666952263378.

4 Quoted in Preves, *Intersex and Identity*, 69.

5 "Updates on Ashley's Story," *Ashley's Blog*, May 8, 2007, http://www .pillowangel.org/updates.htm.

6 *Ashley's Blog*, accessed January 4, 2016, http://www.pillowangel.org.

7 For more about intellectual disability and personhood, see Carey, *On the Margins of Citizenship*; Carlson, *The Faces of Intellectual Disability*; Noll, *Feeble-Minded in Our Midst*; Trent, *Inventing the Feeble Mind*.

8 *Wretches and Jabberers* (dir. Gerardine Wurzburg, 2007). All the following quotes by autistic people come from this film.

9 For more about personhood and communication, see Sequenzia and Grace, *Typed Words, Loud Hands*.

10 Check out the Autistic Self Advocacy Network (http://autisticadvocacy .org) and the network of self-advocates and People First groups in the United States and around the world (http://selfadvocacy.net).

11 Sager, "Just Stories," 196.

10. Promise of Cure

1 I wrote this not having sat with transabled people in community. Rather I have listened to and read their stories in magazines, documentaries, academic journals, and Internet-based forums. I'm sure that my understanding of their experiences and desires would be different and more nuanced if what I knew came through community-based connections.

2 This quote and the following quotes from transabled men come from *Whole* (dir. Melody Gilbert, 2003).

3 Baril, "Transness as Debility," 66.

4 Baril, "Transness as Debility," 71.

5 Annette Marcus has been a good friend and co-conspirator since March 1986, when we sat together at a nonviolence training on the Great Peace March.

6 For a critique of the obesity epidemic, see Rothblum and Solovay, *The Fat Studies Reader*; Campos et al., "The Epidemiology of Overweight and Obesity."

Adichie, Chimamanda Ngozi. "The Danger of a Single Story." TED, July 2009. http://www.ted.com/talks/chimamanda_adichie_the_danger _of_a_single_story?language=en.

Alexander, Michelle. *The New Jim Crow: Mass Incarceration in the Era of Color-blindness*. New York: New Press, 2012.

American Psychiatric Association. *Diagnostic and Statistical Manual of Mental Disorders, Third Edition (DSM-III)*. Washington, DC: American Psychiatric Association, 1987.

———. *Diagnostic and Statistical Manual of Mental Disorders, Fourth Edition, Text Revision (DSM-IV-TR)*. Washington, DC: American Psychiatric Association, 1994.

———. *Diagnostic and Statistical Manual of Mental Disorders, Fifth Edition (DSM-5)*. Arlington, VA: American Psychiatric Association, 2013.

Asch, Adrienne. "Recognizing Death While Affirming Life: Can End of Life Reform Uphold a Disabled Person's Interest in Continued Life?" *Hastings Center Report* 35, no. 6 (November–December 2005): s31–s36.

Barclay, Jennifer. "Mothering the 'Useless': Black Motherhood, Disability, and Slavery." *Women, Gender, and Families of Color* 2, no. 2 (2014): 115–40.

Baril, Alexandre. "Transness as Debility: Rethinking Intersections between Trans and Disabled Embodiments." *Feminist Review*, no. 111 (2015): 59–74.

Bauman, H-Dirksen L., and Joseph J. Murray. *Deaf Gain: Raising the Stakes for Human Diversity*. Minneapolis: University of Minnesota Press, 2014.

Baynton, Douglas C. "Disability and the Justification of Inequality in American History." In *The New Disability History: American Perspectives*, edited by Paul K. Longmore and Lauri Umansky, 33–57. New York: New York University Press, 2001.

Ben-Moshe, Liat, Chris Chapman, and Allison C. Carey, eds. *Disability Incarcerated*. New York: Palgrave Macmillan, 2014.

Black, Edwin. *War against the Weak: Eugenics and America's Campaign to Create a Master Race*. New York: Four Walls Eight Windows, 2003.

Blair, Wendy. "To Raise the Intelligence of the State." Radio broadcast. Aired 1981. Washington, DC: National Public Radio, 1981.

Boster, Dea. *African American Slavery and Disability: Bodies, Property, and Power in the Antebellum South, 1800–1860*. New York: Routledge, 2013.

Bouie, Jamelle. "Michael Brown Wasn't a Superhuman Demon." *Slate*, November 24, 2014. http://www.slate.com/articles/news_and_politics /politics/2014/11/darren_wilson_s_racial_portrayal_of_michael _brown_as_a_superhuman_demon.html.

Bradford, Phillips Verner, and Harvey Blume. *Ota Benga: The Pygmy in the Zoo*. New York: St. Martin's, 1992.

Bromberg, Walter, and Frank Simon. "The 'Protest' Psychosis: A Special Type of Reactive Psychosis." *Archives of General Psychiatry* 19, no. 2 (1968): 155–60.

Burch, Susan. "'Dislocated Histories': The Canton Asylum for Insane Indians." *Women, Gender, and Families of Color* 2, no. 2 (2014): 141–62.

Cameron, Catherine M., Paul Kelton, and Alan C. Swedlund, eds. *Beyond Germs: Native Depopulation in North America*. Tucson: University of Arizona Press, 2015.

Campos, Paul, Abigail Saguy, Paul Ernsberger, Eric Oliver, and Glen Gaesser. "The Epidemiology of Overweight and Obesity: Public Health Crisis or Moral Panic?" *International Journal of Epidemiology* 35, no. 1 (2006): 55–60.

Carey, Allison C. *On the Margins of Citizenship: Intellectual Disability and Civil Rights in Twentieth-Century America*. Philadelphia: Temple University Press, 2009.

Carlson, Licia. *The Faces of Intellectual Disability: Philosophical Reflections*. Bloomington: Indiana University Press, 2010.

Carter, Angela M. "Teaching with Trauma: Disability Pedagogy, Feminism, and the Trigger Warnings Debate." *Disability Studies Quarterly* 35, no. 2 (2015). http://dsq-sds.org/article/view/4652.

Cartwright, Samuel A. "Report on the Diseases and Physical Peculiarities of the Negro Race." *New Orleans Medical and Surgical Journal* (May 1851): 691–715.

Chen, Mel Y. *Animacies: Biopolitics, Racial Mattering, and Queer Affect*. Durham, NC: Duke University Press, 2012.

Child, Brenda. *Boarding School Seasons: American Indian Families, 1900–1945.* Lincoln: University of Nebraska Press, 1998.

Clare, Eli. *Exile and Pride: Disability, Queerness, and Liberation.* Durham, NC: Duke University Press, 2015.

Cohen, Susan, and Christine Cosgrove. *Normal at Any Cost: Tall Girls, Short Boys, and the Medical Industry's Quest to Manipulate Height.* New York: Tarcher/Penguin, 2009.

Cuvier, Georges. *The Animal Kingdom Arranged in Conformity with Its Organization.* London: G. B. Whittaker, 1827.

Daly, Jeff, dir. *Where's Molly: A True Story of Those Lost and Found.* DVD. San Francisco: SFO Productions, 2007.

Dart, Tom. "Texas Teenager Suffering 'Affluenza' Avoids Jail for Second Time." *Guardian*, February 5, 2014. www.theguardian.com/world/2014/feb/06/texas-teenager-affluenza-escapes-jail-second-time.

Deloria, Vine, Jr. *Custer Died for Your Sins: An Indian Manifesto.* 1969. Norman: University of Oklahoma Press, 1988.

Dreger, Alice Domurat. *One of Us: Conjoined Twins and the Future of Normal.* Cambridge, MA: Harvard University Press, 2004.

Erdoes, Richard, and John (Fire) Lame Deer. *Lame Deer, Seeker of Visions.* New York: Simon and Schuster, 1994.

Erevelles, Nirmala, and Andrea Minear. "Unspeakable Offenses: Untangling Race and Disability in Discourses of Intersectionality." *Journal of Literary and Cultural Disability Studies* 4, no. 2 (2010): 127–45.

Ferguson, Philip M., Dianne L. Ferguson, and Meredith M. Brodsky. *"Away from the Public Gaze": A History of the Fairview Training Center and the Institutionalization of People with Developmental Disabilities in Oregon.* Monmouth: The Teaching Research Institute, 2008. http://mn.gov/mnddc/parallels2/pdf/00s/08/08-Fairview_Report.pdf.

Franklin, Ben A. "Authorized Sterilization Leads to Long Search." *Sarasota Herald Tribune*, March 30, 1980.

Gallagher, Hugh Gregory. *FDR's Splendid Deception.* St. Petersburg, FL: Vandamere, 1999.

Gilbert, Melody, dir. *Whole.* DVD. Saint Paul: Frozen Feet Films, 2003.

Gonnerman, Jennifer. "The School of Shock." *Mother Jones* 32, no. 5 (2007): 36–90.

Goode, David, Darryl B. Hill, Jean Reiss, and William Bronston. *History and Sociology of the Willowbrook State School.* Washington, DC: American Association on Intellectual and Developmental Disabilities, 2013.

Green, Michael, and Theda Perdue. *The Cherokee Nation and the Trail of Tears.* New York: Penguin, 2008.

Hershey, Laura. "Translating the Crip." *The Violence of Stairs* (blog), March

6, 2012. http://theviolenceofstairs.tumblr.com/post/18862318185
/translating-the-crip.

Hornblum, Allen M. *Acres of Skin: Human Experiments at Holmesburg Prison.*
New York: Routledge, 1998.

Humphries, Tom, and Carol Padden. *Inside Deaf Culture.* Cambridge, MA:
Harvard University Press, 2005.

Hunter, Margaret. "The Persistent Problem of Colorism: Skin Tone, Status,
and Inequality." *Sociology Compass* 1, no. 1 (2007): 237–54.

Icarus Project. *Navigating the Space between Brilliance and Madness: A Reader
and Roadmap of Bipolar Worlds.* Icarus Project, 2007. Accessed March
2013, http://www.theicarusproject.net/navigating-space-reader-printer
-version-available-online.

Jackson, Vanessa. "In Our Own Voice: African-American Stories of Oppres-
sion, Survival and Recovery in Mental Health Systems." Power2U.org.
Accessed January 13, 2016, https://www.power2u.org/downloads
/InOurOwnVoiceVanessaJackson.pdf.

———. "Separate and Unequal: The Legacy of Racially Segregated Psychiatric Hospitals." PDA. Accessed January 13, 2016, https://www.patdeegan
.com/sites/default/files/files/separate_and_unequal.pdf.

Jacobs, Margaret D. *A Generation Removed: The Fostering and Adoption of
Indigenous Children in the Postwar World.* Lincoln: University of Nebraska
Press, 2014.

Jawort, Adrian. "Genocide by Other Means: U.S. Army Slaughtered Buffalo
in Plains Indian Wars." Indian Country Today, May 9, 2011. http://
indiancountrytodaymedianetwork.com/2011/05/09/genocide-other
-means-us-army-slaughtered-buffalo-plains-indian-wars-30798.

Johnson, Harriet McBryde. *Too Late to Die Young: Nearly True Tales from a
Life.* New York: Picador, 2005.

Johnson, Mary. "Terri Schiavo and the Disability Rights Movement: Activists
Pro, Con on Involvement in Schiavo Case." *Ragged Edge*, November 16,
2003. http://www.raggededgemagazine.com/extra/schiavodisrights.html.

Jordan, William R. *The Sunflower Forest: Ecological Restoration and the New
Communion with Nature.* Berkeley: University of California Press, 2003.

Kaelber, Lutz. "Eugenics: Compulsory Sterilization in 50 American States."
University of Vermont. Updated spring 2011. https://www.uvm.edu
/~lkaelber/eugenics/.

Kafer, Alison. "Compulsory Bodies: Reflections on Heterosexuality and Able-
Bodiedness." *Journal of Women's History* 15, no. 3 (2003): 77–89.

———. *Feminist, Queer, Crip.* Bloomington: Indiana University Press, 2013.

———. "Un/Safe Disclosures: Scenes of Disability and Trauma." *Journal
of Literary and Cultural Disability Studies* 10, no. 1 (2016). doi:10.3828
/jlcds.2016.1

Ladd, Paddy, and Harlan Lane. "Deaf Ethnicity, Deafhood, and Their Relationship." *Sign Language Studies* 13, no. 4 (2013): 565–79.

Largent, Mark A. "'The Greatest Curse of the Race': Eugenic Sterilization in Oregon, 1909–1983." *Oregon Historical Quarterly* 103, no. 2 (2002): 188–209.

Larson, Edward. *Sex, Race, and Science: Eugenics in the Deep South*. Baltimore: Johns Hopkins University Press, 1995.

Laughlin, Harry H. *Eugenical Sterilization in the United States*. Chicago: Psychopathic Laboratory of the Municipal Court of Chicago, 1922.

Lev, Arlene Istar. "Gender Dysphoria: Two Steps Forward, One Step Back." *Clinical Social Work Journal* 41, no. 3 (2013): 288–96.

Lombardo, Paul A. *Three Generations, No Imbeciles: Eugenics, the Supreme Court, and* Buck v. Bell. Baltimore: Johns Hopkins University Press, 2008.

Longmore, Paul K. *Telethons: Spectacle, Disability, and the Business of Charity*. Oxford: Oxford University Press, 2016.

Lunbeck, Elizabeth. *The Psychiatric Persuasion: Knowledge, Gender, and Power in Modern America*. Princeton, NJ: Princeton University Press, 1993.

Mairs, Nancy. *Waist-High in the World: A Life among the Nondisabled*. Boston: Beacon, 1997.

Metzl, Jonathan. *The Protest Psychosis: How Schizophrenia Became a Black Disease*. Boston: Beacon, 2009.

Mingus, Mia. "Medical Industrial Complex Visual." *Leaving Evidence* (blog), February 6, 2015. https://leavingevidence.wordpress.com/2015/02/06/medical-industrial-complex-visual/.

Mire, Amina. "Skin-Bleaching: Poison, Beauty, Power, and the Politics of the Colour Line." *Resources for Feminist Research* 28, nos. 3–4 (2001): 13–38.

Mitchiner, Julie Cantrell, and Marilyn Sass-Lehrer. "My Child Can Have More Choices: Reflections of Deaf Mothers on Cochlear Implants for Their Children." In *Cochlear Implants: Evolving Perspectives*, edited by Raylene Paludneviciene and Irene W. Leigh, 71–95. Washington, DC: Gallaudet University Press, 2011.

Morales, Aurora Levins. *Kindling: Writings on the Body*. Cambridge: Palabrera, 2013.

Morales, Aurora Levins, Qwo-Li Driskill, and Leah Lakshmi Piepzna-Samarasinha. "Sweet Dark Places: Letters to Gloria Anzaldúa on Disability, Creativity, and the Coatlicue State." In *El Mundo Zurdo 2: Selected Works for the Meeting of the Society for the Study of Gloria Anzaldúa*, edited by Sonia Saldívar-Hull, Norma Alarcón, and Rita Urquijo-Ruiz, 77–97. San Francisco: Aunt Lute Books, 2012.

Mostert, Mark P. "Useless Eaters: Disability as Genocidal Marker in Nazi Germany." *Journal of Special Education* 36, no. 3 (2002): 157–70.

Mundy, Liza. "A World of Their Own." In *The Best American Science Writing 2003*, edited by Oliver Sacks, 68–87. New York: HarperCollins, 2003.

Munson, Peggy. "The Invisible Panelist." Paper presented at Queer Disability Conference, San Francisco State University, June 2–3, 2002. http://www .disabilityhistory.org/dwa/queer/paper_munson.html.

Natoli, Jaime L., Deborah L. Ackerman, Suzanne McDermott, and Janice G. Edwards. "Prenatal Diagnosis of Down Syndrome: A Systematic Review of Termination Rates (1995–2011)." *Prenatal Diagnosis* 32, no. 2 (2012): 142–53.

Nestle, Joan. "When Tiredness Gives Way to Tiredness." In *Stricken: Voices from the Hidden Epidemic of Chronic Fatigue Syndrome*, edited by Peggy Munson, 39–42. Binghamton, NY: Haworth, 2000.

Newkirk, Pamela. *Spectacle: The Astonishing Life of Ota Benga.* New York: Amistad, 2015.

Nielsen, Kim E. *A Disability History of the United States.* Boston: Beacon, 2012.

Nixon, Rob. *Slow Violence and the Environmentalism of the Poor.* Cambridge, MA: Harvard University Press, 2013.

Nocella, Anthony J., III, Priya Parmar, and David Stovall, eds. *From Education to Incarceration: Dismantling the School-to-Prison Pipeline.* New York: Peter Lang, 2014.

Noll, Steven. *Feeble-Minded in Our Midst: Institutions for the Mentally Retarded in the South, 1900–1940.* Chapel Hill: University of North Carolina Press, 1995.

Ordover, Nancy. *American Eugenics: Race, Queer Anatomy, and the Science of Nationalism.* Minneapolis: University of Minnesota Press, 2003.

Paludneviciene, Raylene, and Raychelle L. Harris. "Impact of Cochlear Implants on the Deaf Community." In *Cochlear Implants: Evolving Perspectives*, edited by Raylene Paludneviciene and Irene W. Leigh, 3–19. Washington, DC: Gallaudet University Press, 2011.

Pascoe, Peggy. "Miscegenation Law, Court Cases, and Ideologies of 'Race' in Twentieth Century America." *Journal of American History* (June 1996): 44–69.

Poore, Carol. "Disability in Nazi Culture." In *Disability in Twentieth-Century German Culture*, 67–139. Ann Arbor: University of Michigan Press, 2007.

Preves, Sharon E. *Intersex and Identity: The Contested Self.* New Brunswick, NJ: Rutgers University Press, 2003.

Price, Margaret. "The Bodymind Problem and the Possibilities of Pain." *Hypatia* 30, no. 1 (2015): 268–84.

———. *Mad at School: Rhetorics of Mental Disability and Academic Life.* Ann Arbor: University of Michigan Press, 2011.

Ray, Sarah Jaquette. *The Ecological Other: Environmental Exclusion in American Culture.* Tucson: University of Arizona Press, 2013.

Reagan, Leslie. *Dangerous Pregnancies: Mothers, Disabilities, and Abortion in Modern America.* Berkeley: University of California Press, 2010.

Reeve, Matthew, dir. *Christopher Reeve: Hope in Motion.* DVD. New York: Virgil Films, 2007.

Rembis, Michael A. *Defining Deviance: Sex, Science, and Delinquent Girls, 1890–1960*. Champaign: University of Illinois Press, 2012.

Reverby, Susan M. *Examining Tuskegee: The Infamous Syphilis Study and Its Legacy*. Chapel Hill: University of North Carolina Press, 2013.

———, ed. *Tuskegee's Truths: Rethinking the Tuskegee Syphilis Study*. Chapel Hill: University of North Carolina Press, 2012.

Roberts, Dorothy. *Fatal Invention: How Science, Politics, and Big Business Recreate Race in the Twenty-First Century*. New York: New Press, 2012.

———. *Killing the Black Body: Reproduction and the Meaning of Reproductive Liberty*. New York: Vintage, 1998.

Rothblum, Esther, and Sondra Solovay, eds. *The Fat Studies Reader*. New York: New York University Press, 2009.

Rothman, Sheila M., and David J. Rothman. *The Willowbrook Wars: Bringing the Mentally Disabled into the Community*. New Brunswick, NJ: Aldine Transaction, 2005.

Rudacille, Deborah. *The Riddle of Gender: Science, Activism, and Transgender Rights*. New York: Anchor Books, 2005.

Sager, Jill. "Just Stories." In *With the Power of Each Breath: A Disabled Women's Anthology*, edited by Debra Connors and Susan Browne, 191–98. San Francisco: Cleis, 1985.

Samuels, Ellen. "Examining Millie and Christine McKoy: Where Enslavement and Enfreakment Meet." *Signs: Journal of Women in Culture and Society* 37, no. 1 (2011): 53–81.

Savage, Candace. *Prairie: A Natural History*. Vancouver: Greystone Books, 2011.

Schalk, Sami. "Coming to Claim Crip: Disidentification with/in Disability Studies." *Disability Studies Quarterly* 33, no. 2 (2013). doi:http://dx.doi.org/10.18061/dsq.v33i2.3705.

Schlamme, Thomas, dir. *Whoopi Goldberg: Live on Broadway*. VHS. Stamford, CT: Vestron Video, 1985.

Sequenzia, Amy, and Elizabeth J. Grace, eds. *Typed Words, Loud Hands*. Fort Worth, TX: Autonomous Press, 2015.

Shah, Sonia. *The Body Hunters: Testing New Drugs on the World's Poorest Patients*. New York: New Press, 2006.

Showalter, Elaine. *Hystories: Hysterical Epidemics and Modern Media*. New York: Columbia University Press, 1997.

Shreve, Susan. *Warm Springs: Traces of a Childhood at FDR's Polio Haven*. New York: Houghton Mifflin, 2007.

Smits, David D. "The Frontier Army and the Destruction of the Buffalo: 1865–1883." *Western Historical Quarterly* 25, no. 3 (1994): 312–38.

Spiegel, Marjorie. *The Dreaded Comparison: Human and Animal Slavery*. London: Mirror Books, 1988.

Stein, June. "From Activist to 'Passivist': Where Is the Mass Movement." In

Stricken: Voices from the Hidden Epidemic of Chronic Fatigue Syndrome, edited by Peggy Munson, 163–72. Binghamton, NY: Haworth, 2000.

Stevens, Bethany. "Interrogating Transability: A Catalyst to View Disability as Body Art." *Disability Studies Quarterly* 31, no. 4 (2011). http://dsq-sds .org/article/view/1705/1755.

Swanner, Grace. *Saratoga Queen of Spas: A History of the Saratoga Spa and the Mineral Springs of the Saratoga and Ballston Areas*. Utica, NY: North Country Books, 1988.

Taylor, Sunaura. "Beasts of Burden: Disability Studies and Animal Rights." *Qui Parle: Critical Humanities and Social Sciences* 19, no. 2 (2011): 191–222.

Teuton, Sean Kicummah. "Disability in Indigenous North America: In Memory of William Sherman Fox." In *The World of the Indigenous Americas*, edited by Robert Warrior, 569–93. New York: Routledge, 2015.

Thompson, Vilissa. "#DisabilityTooWhite: Making the 'Good Trouble' in Advocacy." *Ramp Your Voice!* (blog), May 26, 2016. http://rampyourvoice .com/2016/05/26/disabilitytoowhite-making-good-trouble-advocacy/.

Trent, James. *Inventing the Feeble Mind: A History of Mental Retardation in the United States*. Berkeley: University of California Press, 1994.

Verner, Samuel Phillips. *Pioneering in Central Africa*. Richmond: Presbyterian Committee of Publication, 1903.

Vogt, Carl. *Lectures on Man: His Place in Creation, and in the History of the Earth*. London: Longman, Green, Longman and Roberts, 1864.

Washington, Harriet A. *Deadly Monopolies: The Shocking Corporate Takeover of Life Itself—And the Consequences for Your Health and Our Medical Future*. New York: Doubleday, 2011.

———. *Medical Apartheid: The Dark History of Medical Experimentation on Black Americans*. New York: Doubleday, 2006.

Wendell, Susan. "Unhealthy Disabled: Treating Chronic Illnesses as Disabilities." *Hypatia* 16, no. 4 (2001): 17–33.

Wiseman, Frederick Matthew. *The Voice of the Dawn: An Autohistory of the Abenaki*. Lebanon, NH: University Press of New England, 2011.

WPATH: World Professional Association for Transgender Health. "The Standards of Care—Historical Compilation of Versions 1–6." Accessed November 26, 2015, http://www.wpath.org/site_store_product.cfm ?store_product=38&display_category=0.

Wurzburg, Gerardine, dir. *Wretches and Jabberers*. DVD. Washington, DC: State of the Art, Inc., 2007.

Yellow Bird, Pemina. "Wild Indians: Native Perspectives on the Hiawatha Asylum for Insane Indians." Power2U.org. Accessed March 20, 2014, http://www.power2u.org/downloads/NativePerspectivesPemina YellowBird.pdf.

Beyond Coal campaign, 55–56, 61–62
bicycling. *See* triking
bioethics, 29, 129, 152–56, 184
bison, 58, 187; massacre of, xix, 15–17, 118, 133–35
Bissonnette, Larry, 157–58
Black. *See* African Americans
body identity integrity disorder, 130
body-mind: definition of, xvi–xvii; individualized, 8–10, 13, 15, 26–28, 56, 69–71, 177–79; loss in relation to, 57–62; reshaping of, 28, 138–39, 142–45, 152–56, 175–83; trouble in relation to, 71–75
Brandon Training School (VT), 157–58
Brattleboro Hydropathic Establishment (VT), 78–80
Bristol-Myers Squibb, 95–96
Brodsky, Meredith, 38
brokenness, xx, 37, 59, 177; experience of, 119–21, 159–61; rejection of stereotypes about disability in relation to, 53, 145, 158; stereotypes about disability in relation to, 5–7, 23, 43
Bromberg, Walter, 24–25, 114
Bronx Zoo (NY), 117–18, 184
Brown, Michael, 24–25
Buck, Carrie, xx–xxi, 103–11
Buck, Doris, 108–9, 196n3
Buck, Emma, 103–4, 106–8, 110–11
Buck v. Bell, 103–11
bullying, 6, 87, 108, 144, 156, 182, 184
Butler, Pierce, 105

Canadian Cystic Fibrosis Foundation, 89
cancer, 13, 26, 55–56, 61–63, 70–71, 76, 87–88, 90, 94, 129
cannibal, 116–17
capitalism, 95–97, 118, 136, 173
care: access to, 48, 54, 60, 62, 69–70, 88, 138, 141, 161–63, 178; cure in relation to, 29, 47–48, 112, 152–56; providers, 136; self-care, xx, 159–60
Cartwright, Samuel, 23–25
case files, xxi, 40, 46, 112–15
Central State Hospital (VA), 107
cerebral palsy, xv, xx, 5, 26, 37–42, 76, 85–87, 91–93, 130, 139, 151–53, 162

charity: fund-raising for, xvi, 11, 86, 88–90, 184; organizations, xvi, 8–10, 75, 86, 89, 142, 184
Chase, Cheryl, 155
Christianity, 5–7, 76, 116; normative identity and, 105, 151, 173
Christopher Reeve: Hope in Motion, 10–12
chronic fatigue immune dysfunction syndrome (CFIDS), 73
cisgender, 138, 151, 163, 173, 180
class, 63–64, 74–75, 96–97, 115, 121, 129, 131–32, 138, 151, 161–62, 193n3, 194n7
classism, xv, xx, 62–63, 157, 173, 183
cochlear implants, 77, 91–93
Cochlear Limited, 92
Cohen, Susan, 75
colonialism, xix, 1, 59, 62, 78, 116–18, 134; and imperialism, 45, 97
comfort, 29, 177–78, 184; body-mind experience of, 72, 175, 180, 183; cure in relation to, 26, 78–80, 153–55; desire for, 45; disability in relation to, 72–73, 166; treatment in relation to, 48. *See also* pain
communication, 28–30, 42, 92–93, 113, 152–55, 157–58, 167, 173, 185–86
community, xv–xvii, xix–xx, 9, 71; deaf people and, 91–94; defect in relation to, 23, 25; disabled people and, 55, 61, 72, 80, 89–90, 99, 161–62; marginalized people and, 163, 181–82; sustaining power of, 12, 63, 131, 141, 159, 166, 178
compassion, 29, 182
conjoined twins, 27–28
cornfield, 14, 16–17, 133–35, 173, 176, 177, 184, 186
Cosgrove, Christine, 75
crip, 80, 131–32, 135–36, 145, 154, 193n7, 194n14
Crippled Children's Division (University of Oregon), 37–38, 162
cure, xv–xvii, xx, 5–6, 8; access versus, 89–90; care in relation to, 29, 47–48, 112, 152–56; comfort in relation to, 26, 78–80, 153–55; death in relation to, 71, 77, 92, 95; defect in relation to, 23–28, 70, 177–79; diagnosis in relation to,

illness, 73; AIDS, 26, 54, 63, 86, 88, 94; asthma, 55–56, 61–62, 184–85; body-mind experience of, 61, 131–32, 135; cancer, 13, 26, 55–56, 61–63, 70–71, 76, 87–88, 90, 94, 129; charity in relation to, 88–90; chronic fatigue immune dysfunction syndrome (CFIDS), 73; chronicity and, xviii, 53, 56, 60–63, 70–71, 73, 76, 85, 131–33, 157; cure in relation to, 69–70, 75; cystic fibrosis, 31, 89, 129; disability in relation to, 61–62; eradication and, 11, 26–27, 56, 95, 179; management in relation to, 70–71; medicalization in relation to, 24–25, 114, 178; multiple chemical sensitivity, 73; multiple sclerosis, 40, 58, 88, 129, 165; muscular dystrophy, 40, 72–75, 86, 91; polio, 79–80, 86, 91, 129; smallpox, 26, 79; stroke, 43, 70, 185; syphilis, 86, 118; trypanosomiasis (African sleeping sickness), 95–96; tuberculosis, 79, 86. *See also* pain
images, medical textbook, 55, 155
imbecility, 39, 105–6, 110–11
immigration: Ellis Island (NY), 23, 39; immigrants and, 75, 108, 110–11, 157; quotas on, 105
imperfection: medicalization of, 23, 56; as way of knowing, xvii, 1, 19, 33, 49, 65, 81, 88, 99, 114, 125, 136, 147, 169, 189
imprisonment, 23, 25, 45–47, 107, 115, 117–18, 123, 157
incarceration, 114, 134. *See also* imprisonment
indigenous people, 45, 79, 134, 157; Abenaki (Nation and Territory), 1, 59–60, 79; cure in relation to, xvi, 108, 112, 157; eastern Dakota (people and Territory), 16, 176, 186; survival of, 60, 79; violence toward, 6, 23, 79, 116–18, 134
individualism, 8–10, 13, 15, 26–28, 56, 177–79
injury, 12, 137, 175
injustice, 13, 56, 60, 62, 64, 187. *See also* discrimination
In Our Care, 40, 46
inspiration: charity in relation to, 88–89;

rejection of stereotype of disabled people as, 186, 190; stereotype of disabled people as, 6–7, 10
institutionalization, xx, 104–15, 144, 155, 157–58; body-mind experience of, 47–48, 120–23; cure and the justification of, 23, 25, 38–39, 42, 87
insurance: health care access and, 44, 93, 120, 122, 138, 141, 161–62; profit-making and, 69, 77
intelligence, 37, 39, 116, 156–58
interdependence, 9, 15, 118, 131–32, 135–36, 144–45. *See also* ecosystem
International Classification of Diseases, 41–43
intersex people, 155, 198n7
intimacy: between body-minds, 72, 180; cure in relation to promise of, 96; with natural world, 33, 88
Ionia State Hospital for the Criminally Insane (MI), 114–15, 184
IQ testing, 37, 39, 156
isolation, 11, 13, 45, 63–64, 131, 163–65; cages for, 40, 47

Johnson, Harriet McBryde, 26, 72
joy, xx, 9, 166
Judge Rotenberg Educational Center (MA), 48, 184
justice. *See* social justice

kinship, 123; diagnosis and, 103, 111; severing of, 115
Klonopin (clonazepam), 136

La Frontera Psychiatric Facility (AZ), 184
Lame Deer, John (Fire) (Lakota), 134
language, 24, 29–30, 39, 44, 45, 184; hate, xx, 6–7, 187, 115–16, 118–19, 154; reclamation of, 131–32; sign, 38, 43, 91–94, 167. *See also* communication
Latinos, 23, 132, 157
Laughlin, Harry, 105
learning disability, 8–9, 55–56
legitimacy, 41, 73
LGBTQ people. *See* queerness
life-saving, 5, 14, 26, 48, 70, 86, 94–95, 183
Lombardo, Paul, 110–11

triggers, xix–xxi, 144, 160

triking, 164–66, 189

trouble, 70–78, 91, 94, 130, 153, 179, 181–83. *See also* diagnosis

trypanosomiasis (African sleeping sickness), 95–96

tuberculosis, 79, 86

Tuskegee Syphilis Study, 118

universities, 37, 87

unnatural: cure in relation to, xvi–xvii, 11, 26; disability as, 6–7, 56–58, 116–18; illogic of, 72, 92, 187; natural versus, 14–17, 53–55; normal and abnormal in relation to, 14–17, 173

U.S. government, 30, 87; bison massacre and, 134; Medicaid, 13, 69, 120; U.S. Food and Drug Administration (FDA), 74–75, 78; U.S. military, 55–56, 69, 88, 137; U.S. Supreme Court, 103–9

vaccination, 71, 77, 91–92, 129

Verner, Samuel, 116–17

Vicodin (acetaminophen and hydrocodone), 161

violence, 11, 13, 63, 110; bison massacre, xix, 15–17, 118, 133–35; colonialism and, 6, 23–25, 41–45, 59–60, 79, 105, 114–19, 134, 173; cure in relation to, 6, 23–32, 70–71, 183; of eradication, 56, 77, 133–35, 156; of genocide, 16, 48, 62, 134–35, 184; of involuntary sterilization, xix–xx, 39–40, 103–12, 134, 153, 155–56; justification of, 23, 47–48, 77, 113, 133, 156; toward the natural world, xx, 16, 55–56, 58–62, 88, 134–35; nuclear families and, 74–75, 103, 119–20, 123, 152–56, 159–60; of physician-assisted suicide, 71, 185; police, 10, 13, 23–25; rape, 40, 103, 159; of suicide, xix–xx, 63–64, 122–23, 159–60, 163, 176; of treatment, 48, 54, 118, 152–56, 162; trigger warnings and, xix–xxi

visions and voices, 42–43, 131, 183; author's experience of, 119–23, 139, 144, 159–60, 169

Vogt, Carl, 116

Voices from Fairview, 47, 113–14

vulnerability, 144–45, 155, 159; stereotypes about, 55

walking, 16–17, 49, 99, 180, 186–87; medical-industrial complex in relation to, 37, 173, 183; rolling versus, 86, 99, 132, 196n1

Washtenaw County Community Mental Health (MI), 122–23

wealth, 11–12, 74–75, 80, 95, 105, 111

weight loss, xvi, 69, 77, 137, 180–83

Wendell, Susan, 61

Where's Molly: A True Story of Those Lost and Found, 40, 46, 113

Whitehead, Irving, 104–5

whiteness, 142–45; cure in relation to, 14, 23–24, 77–80, 86, 111, 129, 154, 179; desire for, 78, 108–9, 111; domination and, 25, 59, 114–18, 134; entitlement and, 6, 9–13, 74–75, 96, 105, 107–8, 155; poverty and, 110; privilege and, 121, 137–38, 151, 161; Western culture and, xvi, 7, 41–45, 71–72, 142, 173, 179

white supremacy, 25, 77–78; resistance to, 9–10, 24, 114

Whole, 175–76

wholeness, xvii, 158–59, 174–77

Whoopi Goldberg: Live on Broadway, 143

Willowbrook State School (NY), 118

Wilson, Darren, 24–25

witnessing, 56, 59–60, 163, 181

Wood, Paul, 47

work, 47, 62, 143, 166, 174; of activism, 13–14, 48, 158, 181–82; of cure, 28, 56, 70, 85–97, 173; disabling conditions of, 62; of restoration, 14–17; of treatment, 9–13, 53, 73–74

World Health Organization, 96

Wretches and Jabberers, 157–58

yearning: cure in relation to, 57–58, 94, 155, 176, 180; experience of, 37, 58–60, 62, 88, 103–7, 110–11, 113, 115, 156, 175. *See also* longing

Zero Fatalities campaign, 129

Zoe's Race, 89–90